Philosophy Tips For Living Everyday Life

Jennifer L. Whitfield

Introduction

Welcome to this book, a journey into the profound wisdom and practical applications of philosophy in our daily existence. Philosophy, often considered an abstract and esoteric discipline, is, in fact, deeply relevant to the questions and challenges we encounter in our everyday lives. This guide aims to bridge the gap between philosophy and practicality, offering insights and tools to help you navigate life's complexities with greater clarity, wisdom, and fulfillment.

The examined life lies at the heart of philosophy. In this guide, we will embark on a journey of self-reflection and introspection, exploring fundamental questions about our beliefs, values, and the nature of reality. We will delve into the art of critical thinking, equipping you with the tools to question assumptions, challenge biases, and navigate the complex landscape of information and ideas.

Truth and honesty are pillars of philosophical inquiry, and we will explore the concept of truth and its consequences in our daily lives. We will discuss the nature of honesty and deception, inviting you to reflect on the ethical implications of our words and actions.

Developing the capacity for clear and logical thinking is a valuable skill in our information-rich world. We will delve into the principles of rationality, reasoning, and logical argumentation, empowering you to think critically and make sound judgments in various domains of life.

Philosophy is intimately connected to our personal identity and values. We will explore the concept of personal identity, inviting you to reflect on your own identity and the factors that shape your sense of self. Additionally, we will discuss the importance of principles and ethical frameworks in guiding our actions and decisions.

Amidst the consumerist culture that often dominates our lives, we will delve into the concept of materialism and its limitations. By examining the deeper meaning of life and exploring alternative sources of fulfillment, we will uncover ways to cultivate a more meaningful and purpose-driven existence.

Language is a powerful tool that shapes our thoughts, perceptions, and interactions. We will explore the role of language in constructing meaning and understanding, inviting you to reflect on the power of words and the importance of effective communication in fostering meaningful connections with others.

The guide will also touch upon profound existential questions about life and death, urging you to confront the transient nature of our existence and find meaning within it. By contemplating our mortality and embracing the impermanence of life, we can cultivate a deeper appreciation for the present moment and make choices aligned with our values and aspirations.

Throughout the guide, we will revisit the concept of the examined life, encouraging you to continuously reflect, question, and challenge your assumptions and beliefs. Philosophy is not merely an abstract pursuit but a practical guide for living, helping us navigate the complexities of our existence with wisdom, compassion, and a deeper understanding of ourselves and the world around us.

By engaging with the principles and practices presented in this guide, you will have the opportunity to transform your everyday life, gaining valuable insights and tools to navigate challenges, make informed decisions, and lead a more meaningful and fulfilling existence. Philosophy invites us to embrace the richness of the human experience and invites us to live with greater intention, authenticity, and purpose.

Now, let us embark on this extraordinary journey into the realm of practical philosophy, where profound insights meet everyday life. Prepare to expand your horizons, challenge your assumptions, and discover the transformative power of philosophy in shaping your existence. The wisdom of the ages is within your reach, and this guide will serve as your trusted companion on this remarkable quest for knowledge, meaning, and self-discovery. Let us begin this adventure into the practical wisdom of philosophy for everyday life.

Contents

1. The examined life

The unexamined life is not worth living.

Socrates

Philosophy invites us to examine our lives, and offers us the means of doing so. By becoming more aware of what we believe, we can challenge our beliefs and, if we wish, change them.

Socrates was one of the most famous philosophers of all time and he spent a lot of his own time going around annoying people. Philosophers, and philosophy, can be annoying. It's easy to become comfortable with the ideas and opinions we have, whether they are right or wrong. If they are challenged, we may begin to feel very uncomfortable. What Socrates discovered was that if you persistently question people about things they think they know, even if they are supposed to be experts on the subject, they often find it difficult to come up with satisfactory explanations or justifications. Unsurprisingly, few people in Athens thanked him for his troubles and he became very unpopular amongst certain sections of Athenian society. Although he was by no means the first philosopher, he seems to have been the first to make constant questioning the basis of his approach. It was through constant questioning that Socrates examined both his own life and the lives of others.

Socrates (469–399 BC)
Most important works: he wrote nothing himself, but his pupil Plato wrote a lot about him.

Socrates became a hero to his followers, but his enemies managed to get him condemned to death in Athens for 'corrupting the minds of the young'. He died by drinking hemlock. The name of his wife, Xanthippe, has since become a word that means a bad-tempered woman!

Philosophy helps us to examine our lives by questioning what we think, what we believe and what we claim to know. By challenging our ideas and beliefs, demanding that we reflect on them, philosophy makes us more aware of why we have them. It is very easy to express an opinion, much harder to justify it. We pick up a lot of ideas and beliefs on our way though life and, like habits, we can acquire bad ones as well as good ones. It can become all too easy to forget how or why we picked them up, and some may have been with us for so long that we forget we ever actually *acquired* them at all. It may feel as if they have always been with us.

Once we begin to reflect on our beliefs, we may find it difficult to justify some of them even to ourselves! For example, most people who vote in elections tend to vote for the same party each time. The number of people who switch their votes from one party to another is quite small. When we voted for the first time we may have gone through a lengthy process of deliberation, but by the tenth time it may have become more a matter of habit. But what seemed like a good reason to vote for a particular party when we were twenty might not seem like such a good one when we are 60. When we think about it, we may find that we can no longer remember, or, if we can remember, no longer agree with, the reasons why we hold various views. As we go through life we may change the way we look, but we often forget to change the way we think.

Once we realize that we have acquired something we also realize that we might *not* have done so. Once we realize that something is optional, we also realize that we are free to accept or reject it. In this sense, philosophy is liberating because through giving us greater awareness of our ideas and beliefs it also gives us greater control over them. You do not have to be a prisoner of your own past. Once you become aware that you have made a decision, you also become aware that you can change your mind, just as you can change the way you look.

By challenging the ideas and beliefs we know we have, we may also bring to the surface others that have long lurked below the threshold of our awareness. Our lives are routinely shaped by a whole raft of assumptions we may never have consciously even thought about. Many of these will have been acquired when we were children. Until we become fully aware of them we cannot begin to examine them, and until we examine them we cannot decide whether or not we really agree with them. Philosophy is not like psychoanalysis. I am not talking about ideas that we have repressed because we feel guilty about them. What I am talking about is ideas that we seem to have always had. These ideas shape our view of what is 'natural' and 'normal'. (→ 15)

Once we have examined what we think, what we believe and what we claim to know, we may come to see the world, and perhaps ourselves as well, quite differently. If we have removed errors and inconsistencies, if we have discarded ideas that we have come to see as unjustifiable, we should see the world not only differently but also better. Socrates saw the examined life as not just an option, but also as an improvement. If we have a better grasp of things then we should live better lives. A basic principle that underlies the approach I am taking in this book is that our beliefs shape our perceptions and our perceptions shape our actions. Few people need persuading that it is a good idea to get out of a house that is on fire. Once we can see that it is on fire there is not much to think about in terms of what to do. If we see things differently, we will respond to them differently. In honour of Socrates, your first exercise is a famous philosophical puzzle associated with him.

The Euthyphro dilemma is named after someone who is interrogated by Socrates in Plato's dialogue of the same name. The problem Socrates confronts Euthyphro with is this: do the gods love what is good because it is good, or is it the fact that they love it that makes something good?

The initial implications of the dilemma are quite straightforward. If (a) the gods love what is good because it is good, then whatever is good is good independently of what the gods feel about it. If, on the other hand, (b) something is good because the gods love it, then they could equally well love something else instead.

If (a) is the case, then the gods have no role to play in establishing the foundations of moral values. If (b) is the case, they have a role to play, but what is good turns out to be nothing more than what they happen to love. If (a) is the case, morality is independent of religion. If (b) is the case, morality is highly unstable (the ancient Greek gods were notoriously fickle!).

Dilemmas are only problematic if neither outcome is attractive. Atheists would not be troubled by this one because they could happily accept the implications of (a) and not care about (b). However, the dilemma is highly problematic for those who want to base moral values on religion, because neither half of the dilemma feels comfortable.

At the end of Plato's dialogue, Euthyphro simply makes his excuses and leaves. He has had quite enough of the examined life for one day. However, the Euthyphro dilemma is still relevant, and relevant to everyday life. For example, many people say that morality is in decline because religion is in decline, and that a revival of the one would lead to a revival of the other. The Euthyphro dilemma poses a serious challenge to that view. Is something morally good because a particular religion approves of it, or does a particular religion approve of it because it is morally good? The dilemma also has a wider application. For example, is a work of art good because people like it, or do they like it because it is good? Is a style of clothing fashionable because a lot of people wear it, or do a lot of people wear it because it is fashionable?

See if you can think of other examples of the Euthyphro dilemma. Are there things you approve of because other people approve of them?

Philosophy, if it cannot answer so many questions as we would wish, has at least the power of asking questions which increase the interest of the world, and show the strangeness and wonder lying just below the surface even in the commonest things of life.
Bertrand Russell

2. I don't believe it!

Never believe what you cannot doubt.

Robin Skelton

If you believe everything you hear, you are a mug – sooner or later every con artist in the area will beat a path to your door. But how do you decide what to believe and what not to believe? That is the problem. And philosophers have been trying to solve it for centuries.

There is no point in asking questions if we are simply going to believe any answer that we are given. Equally, there is no point in asking questions if we are simply going to *disbelieve* any answer that we are given. How do we strike the right balance in everyday life between gullibility and incredulity? Although this is a problem that has to be faced by all philosophers, the experts in the area of doubt are the Sceptics.

Scepticism has a long history. There is a theory that it originated in India and was brought to Europe by Pyrrho of Elis (c.360–c.270 BC). Whether or not this is true, Pyrrho is usually regarded as the founder of Western Scepticism, and so ancient Scepticism is sometimes called Pyrrhonism in his honour. The Greek word 'sceptic' originally simply meant an enquirer. Pyrrhonism is sometimes distinguished from what is called modern Scepticism, which is usually taken to begin with Descartes. There are important differences between the two, and both of them will be looked at in this chapter.

René Descartes (1596–1650)

Most important works: *Discourse on Method, Meditations on the First Philosophy*

Descartes served in the army for several years. He died in Sweden, having been invited there to be tutor to Queen Christina. He liked to stay in bed all morning but she insisted on starting their lessons at 5 am!

The form of Scepticism associated with Descartes is sometimes called 'systematic doubt'. He invented a thought-experiment to find out whether there were any limits to what he could doubt. Here is the same experiment for you to try …

Descartes set out to discover whether he could doubt absolutely everything. He imagined that there was an evil demon whose only role and pleasure in life was deceiving him. This would mean that however certain something seemed, it might just be a case of the

demon deceiving him. In the end, however, Descartes discovered something that he could not doubt, however powerful or cunning the demon might be. Do you think there is anything that you could not possibly doubt?

Descartes famously discovered that the one thing he could not doubt was his ability to think. He expressed this discovery in Latin as '*Cogito ergo sum*', meaning 'I think therefore I am!' He could not doubt his own existence, because he had to exist in order to be able to doubt it! However, it was not just doubting that confirmed his own existence. Any kind of thinking had the same result, because he had to exist in order to think. Even if he believed something that was completely wrong, he had to exist in order to believe it.

Descartes' experiment was just that, an experiment. For Descartes, the experiment ended not in doubt but in certainty. Having convinced himself that he existed, he then managed to convince himself that God existed too, and that gave him all the foundations for knowledge that he needed. Others have been less convinced; far from putting the matter to bed, many who came after Descartes felt he had demonstrated the power of doubt without discovering the antidote for it.

Descartes raised the issue of when it is *possible* to doubt, and the fact is that it is almost always possible. However, modern critics of Scepticism have tended to focus on a different question: when is it *reasonable* to doubt? Just because I *can* do something does not mean that it is reasonable for me to do so. Just because I *can* drive a van quickly through a busy pedestrian precinct does not make it a good idea, in fact I can think of a number of compelling reasons why I should not do it.

Where are you reading this? Can you think of a good reason to doubt that you are actually there? If so, what is it? If not, can you think of what a good reason might be?

I shall assume that most readers do not seriously doubt where they are at this moment and so I shall focus on the last part of the question. Why might I doubt that I really am where I think I am? One obvious possibility is that I might be dreaming. In that case I would actually be in my bed, but the location of my dream, where I seem to be when I am reading this, would be somewhere else. However, it does not normally take me very long to establish whether I am awake or not, so my doubt, even if reasonable, is unlikely to last very long either.

It is fairly easy to think of circumstances in which doubt is unreasonable. It is more difficult to say how much doubt *is* reasonable. Ancient Sceptics like Pyrrho took a rather different line that avoided having to confront this problem. To them it seemed obvious that we tend to believe things on the basis of inadequate evidence and that this is a bad habit. They believed that if we cannot be sure about something, then the only rational response is to refrain from forming an opinion about it. They were not so much concerned that we might be wrong, but that we might be unhappy. Forming an opinion that may turn out to be incorrect is setting yourself up to be disappointed. Because we do not *need* to form opinions, we can avoid being disappointed. Forming opinions is a potential source of unnecessary suffering because we become attached to the opinions we form. The ancient Sceptic way of putting this was that we should 'suspend judgement' on things. The story was told that Pyrrho had to be followed around by his friends just in case he 'suspended his judgement' concerning whether he was on the edge of a cliff or not and fell off it! Since Pyrrho lived to a ripe old age, the story is either totally untrue or else Pyrrho had a lot of friends with a lot of time on their hands.

Pyrrho of Elis (c.360–c.270 BC)
Most important works: he is not known to have written anything.

Pyrrho spent most of his life in southern Greece, and may have been a painter for a while. He travelled to Persia and India with the army of Alexander the Great.

However, that story about Pyrrho reflects a basic problem with Scepticism: the suspension of judgement makes everyday life look almost impossible. If there is no reason for doing this rather than that, how are we to decide anything? We seem to be in the position of Buridan's ass. (→ 10) Fortunately, the Sceptics were sensible enough to see both the problem and a solution to it. Where we cannot be certain we go with the most likely option, and the most likely option is the one most people subscribe to. So if most people think that something is a cliff, then for practical purposes that is the option to go with. Consequently, and perhaps a little surprisingly, although their philosophical position was a radical one, the Sceptics were generally conformists, because they would tend to side with the majority.

What the ancient Sceptics latched onto was the fact that we habitually create problems for ourselves, so the solution to those problems is simply to stop creating them. If there is no need to take a strong position on something where the evidence at best supports a weak one, then there is no point in doing so. The Sceptics did not argue that we can never know anything, only that we should demand incontrovertible evidence before we give our agreement to something. In their view, this was unlikely ever to happen, but they could not rule it out. For practical purposes this did not matter because we do not need incontrovertible evidence in order to live. If everyone is eating the same food and no one is showing any signs of being poisoned, that is good enough for me. If I wait for incontrovertible evidence that the food in front of me is not poisoned before I eat it, the most likely outcome is that I shall die of starvation. For the ancient Sceptics, suspending judgement did not make life impossible, it just made it much less stressful.

Scepticism should not be confused with uncertainty as such. For example, the uncertainty principle in physics, as developed by Werner Heisenberg, states that some things *cannot* be known, even in theory. That view belongs neither to ancient Scepticism, with its suspension of judgement, nor to modern Scepticism, with its systematic doubt. It belongs to dogmatism, because it makes a categorical claim that something is the case. What Scepticism does is invite us to challenge; it does not require us to deny. Not believing everything we hear (or read) is always good advice.

The next time you read a story in the newspaper, ask yourself 'Should I believe it, or have I good reason to doubt it?' And then 'Does it really matter whether I believe it or not?' The ancient

Sceptics thought that the suspension of judgement made life less stressful. Try it out for yourself and see if it works.

Life is doubt.

Miguel de Unamuno

3. Would I lie to you?

What is truth?

Pontius Pilate

In the story of George Washington and the cherry tree young George exclaims that he 'cannot tell a lie'. If that is true then he was a very unusual person – most people can, although some seem to find it easier than others. And if the truth causes needless harm, is a lie necessarily a bad thing? But what if we all told lies all the time?

Truth is a major topic in philosophy, but in the end there are only two important questions to ask about it. First, what is it? Second, what should we do with it? The first question is too complex and theoretical to even try to address here, but the second one has a lot to do with everyday life.

Fortunately, for practical purposes, we generally know whether we are married or not, how old we are, where we live, how much money we have in the bank, and so on. In practice, we rarely struggle to establish the truth on such everyday matters, in fact, we may sometimes seek to avoid it! Indeed, social life may sometimes rely on its avoidance. In 'Reginald on Besetting Sins', a short story by Saki, we read the sobering tale of 'the woman who told the truth'. As a result of this dangerous habit, she loses her friends, her

13

dressmaker and her cook. It is easy to say that people should always tell the truth, but as soon as we begin to reflect on the matter we realize that we do not really believe that. In fact, truth-telling is bound up in a complex network of conventions and assumptions.

Here is an illustration of what I mean from personal experience. When I was travelling in Kashmir in the 1980s I was introduced to the concept of 'business talk'. Business talk meant that it was permissible to tell lies when you were buying and selling. Although it was never explicitly stated, the reason seemed to be that no one really took seriously what was said in the haggling process, so no one was really deceived. No one ever really thought that the carpet seller's wife and children would be sold into slavery if the asking price were not forthcoming, or that the prospective purchaser really had no money whatsoever. Exaggeration of one kind or another was merely part of the ritual, and as long as something was said as part of that ritual it was exempt from the normal rules of truth-telling. As long as everyone knows and plays by the same rules, it can be argued that no damage is done by this way of doing things. However, the unwary tourist who does not know the rules and plays by different ones may clearly be disadvantaged. That is the point about conventions: they have to be learned. They are not obvious or 'natural'.

Draw up a list of three things you think it is permissible to lie about. Try not to make them too general – 'money' is too vague; 'filling in a tax return' is more suitable. Once you have your list, think of at least one reason why you think it is acceptable to lie about that thing.

Obviously different people will come up with different permissible lies and different reasons, so the discussion of this exercise has to proceed in very general terms. Typically justifications for telling lies fall into two broad categories. Either the lies told are regarded as trivial, or they are told specifically in order to avoid causing harm.

Exactly what makes a lie 'trivial' is not at all easy to pin down. For example, it may have to do with the subject matter, it may have to do with the closeness (or otherwise) of the person to whom the lie is told. More cynically, the chances of being caught out may shape our views of what is or is not to be regarded as 'trivial'.

Harm may come in various shapes and sizes, but when it comes to telling lies it is often emotional harm that is in the forefront of our thoughts. More cynically, again, it may be the avoidance of harm to ourselves that is in the back of our minds more than the harm we might cause to others.

The two categories may overlap, in that the degree of triviality involved in telling a lie might be measured by the level of harm it avoids. It is only when we become honest with ourselves about when we think it is permissible to tell lies that we can properly examine and evaluate our reasons for doing so. Or, finally, we may believe that it is never permissible to tell a lie under any circumstances.

As with 'business talk' some lies may just be a matter of social convention and so be expected rather than condemned. Some may be so expected that they are not even thought of as lies, merely good manners. Unless you are seeking medical advice, the question 'How are you?' rarely expects the truth in return, and replying with the truth, the whole truth and nothing but the truth may be taken as an indication that you fail to understand the convention. (→ 12)

Here is something else to think about. Someone I once worked with used to say, 'If my lips are moving, I'm lying.' He meant it as a joke (I think!). But if he meant it seriously, what is he really saying?

This is a modern variation on a very old theme, often referred to as the 'Cretan liar' problem. A man from Crete tells you that Cretans always tell lies. If he is telling the truth, then Cretans always tell lies. But if he is a Cretan, he must be lying. That means that he is lying and telling the truth at the same time. If the person who says, 'When my lips are moving, I'm lying' is telling the truth, then he is also lying, because his lips are moving! The difficulty in both cases stems from the fact that people are talking directly or indirectly about themselves (this is called 'self-reference'). If I am not from Crete and I say that Cretans always tell lies, then the same difficulty does not arise.

Not telling the truth is not the same thing as telling lies. I may not tell the truth for a variety of reasons, of which ignorance is probably the most common. When I lie I am *aware* that I am not telling the truth. Because they have generally been fixated on the truth, relatively few philosophers have addressed themselves to the subject of lying. An honourable exception can be found in the shape of Montaigne's essay 'On Liars'.

Michel de Montaigne (1533–1592)
Most important work: *Essays*

Lawyer, landowner and for some time mayor of Bordeaux, Montaigne wrote about many different topics, exploring his own views of them. He admired the ancient philosophers, especially the Stoics and the Sceptics. He had a medal made for himself with the inscription 'What do I know?' on it.

Montaigne points out that lying requires imagination, because a lie has to be created. Moreover, liars need to have good memories in order to remember what they have created. In order to minimize the risk of being caught out, it is best if the lie is significantly different from the truth, so as to avoid confusing the one with the other. It is also advisable to lie consistently – those who change their stories on a regular basis may find themselves in the company of two or more people who have heard two or more different stories, and that could prove awkward!

The reason why telling lies as a matter of politeness or as part of a ritual of negotiation is acceptable to many people is because no deception is intended, and that is essentially a moral reason. However, there is another kind of reason why lying is problematic.

Telling lies as a matter of routine undermines the basic principles of human communication. Telling lies only makes sense because we generally assume that most people normally tell the truth (→ 24). But what if no one *ever* told the truth? If all Cretans really *were* liars, they would have found it very difficult to communicate with each other. As Montaigne points out, 'the opposite of a truth has a hundred thousand shapes'. Imagine two liars having a conversation: one says, 'I live in London', and the other replies, 'So do I.' The only thing we know for sure is that neither of them lives in London; where they actually do live is anyone's guess. If we want to communicate, then the truth is an efficient vehicle for doing so, a lie is not.

The next time you feel tempted to tell a lie, stop! Think about it. What is your reason for lying? Is it a good reason? If it is not, then think again.

There are three kinds of lies: lies, damned lies and statistics!
Benjamin Disraeli

4. Thinking straight

'Contrariwise,' continued Tweedledee, 'if it was so, it might be; and if it were so, it would be: but as it isn't, it ain't. That's logic.'
Lewis Carroll

There are things that some people do better than others, and one of those things is thinking. The better the quality of our thinking, the better the quality of our decision making is likely to be. And the better the quality of our decision making, the better our quality of life is likely to be. Logic helps us to think better and so helps deliver a better quality of life. Logic helps us to think straight and so avoid making mistakes.

This book is not a course in philosophy. Nevertheless, logic is so central to philosophy, to how philosophical thinking works (or is meant to), that it is impossible simply to leave it to one side: this chapter provides a brief introduction. There are various kinds or branches of logic. One branch is called inductive logic (→ 8), while the one looked at in this chapter is called deductive logic.

The theory is that if we follow the rules of logic, if we reason correctly, it should be impossible for us to entertain two incompatible beliefs at the same time. Logic does not tell us what is true or false, but rather what cannot be true if something else is true, or what has to be true if something else is true. A logically valid argument is 'truth preserving', not truth creating. If you put true statements into a valid argument structure, you will get a true conclusion out of it. It is easiest to illustrate this by way of an example. Here is a classic one:

Example 1
Premise 1: All men are mortal.
Premise 2: Socrates is a man.
Conclusion: Socrates is mortal.

What we have here is comprised of both form and content. The content is provided by the specifics (men, mortality, Socrates), the form by the structure into which they are introduced. It is easier to see the structure of the argument if it is stripped down to its bare essentials:

All As are Bs.
X is an A.
Therefore X is a B.

However, it is probably easier to understand this if we rephrase it a little:

If something is an A, it is a B.
This is an A.
Therefore this is a B.

Or again:

If something belongs to group A (e.g. men) it also belongs to group B (e.g. mortal beings)
This thing belongs to group A
Therefore this thing belongs to group B.

Set out this way, it is obvious that the argument is a valid one, and it is sound, independent of whatever true content we assign to A and B. So:

Example 2
Premise 1: All men are goldfish.
Premise 2: Socrates is a man.
Conclusion: Socrates is a goldfish.

It is important to see that this argument has the same form as Example 1. Even though we might disagree with premise 1 and with the conclusion, we must still acknowledge that *if* all men are goldfish *and* Socrates is a man *then* Socrates is a goldfish. The *form* of the argument is valid, but the fact that an argument is valid does not mean that its conclusion is true. *That* requires the premises to be true too.

Consider a third example:

Example 3
Premise 1: All men are mortal.
Premise 2: Socrates is a man.
Conclusion: Socrates is a philosopher.

The premises are true *and* the conclusion is true *but* the argument is invalid. To see why this is so, we can strip the argument down to its bare bones:

All As are Bs
X is an A
Therefore X is a C

The 'C' that appears in the conclusion does not appear anywhere in the premises, which deal only with 'A' and 'B' and 'X'. Premises that tell us nothing about 'C' cannot yield a valid conclusion about 'C', therefore *all* arguments of this form are invalid.

The key point to remember about logic is the difference between truth and validity, between content and form.

The kind of argument we have just been looking at is called a syllogism, and the basic work on it was done by Aristotle. The 'all As are Bs, X is an A, therefore X is a B' form is perhaps the simplest to recognize as valid. There are other forms including premises such as 'some As are Bs' and 'some As are not Bs' where it is a bit harder to tell. Aristotle systematically worked through all the possible combinations to see which were valid and which were invalid. Although the syllogism is a very limited and in some ways a primitive form of argument, it is a very useful place to start. Because it is simple, it makes it relatively easy to learn that there is a fundamental difference between truth and validity.

Aristotle (384–322 BC)
Most important works: *Ethics, Politics, Metaphysics*

A pupil of Plato, Aristotle studied and wrote on a wide range of topics including the weather and animals. He spent some time as the tutor to Alexander the Great and founded his own school called the Lyceum.

Here are some examples of syllogisms for you to have a go at. In each case you need to consider whether the argument is valid. You may find it useful to strip the arguments down to their bare bones, as illustrated above, in order to see the structures of them more clearly.

Premise 1: All men are mortal.
Premise 2: Socrates is mortal.
Conclusion: Therefore Socrates is a man.

This argument is invalid. It may be tempting to think it is valid because the premises and conclusion are all true. However, look at it again when different content is put into the same structure:

Premise 1: All women are mortal.
Premise 2: Socrates is mortal.
Conclusion: Therefore Socrates is a woman.

Why is the argument invalid? Because what premise 1 tells us is that if you belong to group A (women) then you also belong to group B (mortal). But it does not tell us that you must belong to group A in order to belong to group B. So Socrates can belong to group B without belonging to group A. He can be mortal without being a woman.

Would the argument remain invalid if the first premise were changed to 'Only women are mortal'?

No, the argument would then be valid but false. 'Only women are mortal' is another way of saying 'All mortals are women', because if only women are mortal it is impossible to be mortal without being a woman. The argument would then have the valid form:

Premise 1: All mortals are women
Premise 2: Socrates is mortal

Conclusion: Therefore Socrates is a woman.

Here is another example for you to try. Because it deals with 'some' rather than 'all', it is a bit more complicated.

> *Premise 1: Some philosophy books are expensive.*
> *Premise 2: Some expensive books are a waste of money.*
> *Conclusion: Therefore some philosophy books are a waste of money.*

This may all sadly be true, but the argument is invalid again. Suppose we have twenty expensive books. Ten of them could be philosophy books and the other ten could be a waste of money. We have no way of knowing, on the basis of what we have been told, that any of them are both.

If you have grasped the distinction between truth and validity, you have learned a basic principle of logic. However, the syllogism is obviously a very limited kind of argument and everyday life is likely to present us with many occasions where we cannot use it. Fortunately, logic has a lot more to offer. As well as other much more complicated systems of logic that we cannot go into here, logicians have also identified a number of *fallacies*. A fallacy is a mistake in logic. If we find one in an argument, we know that the argument is not valid. Here are some well-known fallacies to look out for both in your own thinking and in the thinking of others. Many have traditional Latin names attached to them. Use them and impress your friends!

ad hominem The Latin term *ad hominem* means 'against the person'. If we reject the truth of a claim just because of who made it, we are guilty of using an *ad hominem* argument. ('How can you believe a person who …?') The opposite of an *ad hominem* argument is an appeal to authority. Not all appeals to authority are inappropriate, but deciding who is a reliable authority is not always easy. In everyday life, people we admire are sometimes wrong and people we revile are sometimes right.

ad populum This is another Latin term meaning an appeal 'to the people'. The implication is that if everyone agrees, it must be right. Leaving aside the fact that everyone might not agree, even if they did that would not in itself make anything right. When everyone believed that the world was flat, they were wrong. The truth is not decided by a show of hands (even if an election is).

complex question A famous example of a complex question is, 'When did you stop beating your wife?' A complex question is not so much a fallacy as a logical trap. I cannot answer the question as it is put to me without admitting that I beat, or have beaten, my wife. If I say when I stopped, then I admit I used to beat her, and if I say I have not stopped, then I am still doing it!

false dilemma A false dilemma is another kind of trap. 'Do you want to take this medication or do you want to die?' The trap lies in forcing someone to choose between only two options when in fact there are other options available. I do not want to take the medication *or* die, and perhaps it is perfectly possible to do neither (maybe by taking a *different* medication). Politicians often make use of these: vote for us or see the country go to the dogs!

post hoc ergo propter hoc This is not as painful as it sounds! The Latin phrase simply means 'after this therefore because of this'. Just because events take place close to each other does not mean that there is any actual causal connection between them. A lot of superstitions may fall into this category. Bad luck may follow seeing a black cat, but that does mean that the black cat caused the bad luck.

non sequitur In many ways this is *the* logical fallacy. The Latin term simply means 'it does not follow', and this is true of many supposed 'arguments'. 'I am rich, therefore I am a good person to run this country.' Why? 'I am old, therefore I am wise.' Why? 'You are poor, therefore you deserve to be.' Why? Just because two statements are made in the vicinity of each other does not mean that there is any actual connection between them. The ***ad hominem, ad populum*** and ***post hoc ergo propter hoc*** fallacies can all be seen as particular examples of the ***non sequitur*** fallacy.

Logic is not some kind of magical formula that will tell us everything we need to know about everyday life. What it can offer is a set of skills to help us tell the difference between a good argument and a bad one. That alone will improve our thinking about life and help us make better decisions.

Like all skills, thinking takes practice. Unfortunately, life does not divide itself neatly into syllogisms so the scope for practising them is limited. Fallacies, however, are all around us. Be on the lookout for them constantly. Whenever someone says 'This because of that', or 'This therefore that', ask yourself, 'Is there any real connection between this and that?' The examples given above may help you.

Logic is not the knowledge of the use or construction of arguments, but rather the knowledge of discerning and judging them correctly, namely, why some are strong and others weak.

Peter Abelard

5. What's the difference?

Half the wrong conclusions at which mankind arrive are reached by the abuse of metaphors, and by mistaking general resemblance or imaginary similarity for real identity.

Lord Palmerston

If I have my car repaired and they replace some parts, do I get the same car back? Does it matter? If I take my child into hospital for a heart transplant, do I get the same child back? Does it matter? If I give someone a painting to be valued and receive an exact forged copy in return, do I get the same painting back? Does it matter? Does it make a difference whether it is my car, my child or my painting? Should it?

The 'Law of Identity' is often regarded as a fundamental principle of logic. (→ 4) However, to say that 'something is itself' may sound like an unhelpful answer to a question no one needs to ask – and perhaps it is. A rather more interesting question is, 'When does something *stop* being itself?' If that still sounds obscure, then consider the following: at first sight, a caterpillar is one thing and a butterfly another. But a caterpillar can develop into a butterfly. However, a caterpillar that has become a butterfly is no longer a caterpillar. If we have five butterflies and five caterpillars in a box, we do not say we have ten caterpillars. But if we leave them there long enough we may end up with ten butterflies. Here is a classic conundrum that is based on this kind of problem. It is called 'The Ship of Theseus'.

Theseus had a ship built for him. Over time it needed constant repair, with old planks being taken from it and new ones used to replace them. Eventually not a single one of the original planks was left. Did Theseus still have the same ship he started with?

There is no agreed solution to this conundrum. It gets even more complicated if you add in the possibility that someone takes away all the old timbers and builds another ship with them. You would then have two different ships, both of which would have a claim to being 'the ship of Theseus'. Those familiar with BBC television's *Only Fools and Horses* may have encountered the same conundrum in the shape of Trigger's broom. Trigger has had the same broom for years, but he has changed both its head and its handle from time to time. So, if someone had saved all the discarded parts, there might now be several different contestants for the title of 'Trigger's broom'. Is 'Trigger's broom', then, simply the broom that belongs to Trigger *now*? If so, is it a matter of ownership rather than identity? And is 'the ship of Theseus' simply the ship that Theseus happens to possess at any given moment?

All this may seem irrelevant or far-fetched. What has it to do with everyday life? Consider this question: what makes you you? Are you the same as you were last year? Or ten years ago? Physically, there are parts of you that are constantly being replaced. The cells in your skin have a lifecycle that can be measured in weeks. Blood cells have an even faster turnover, while you may have had some of the cells in your internal organs for years! Mentally, we learn things, we forget things, we mature and we age. External events can shape our lives in all kinds of ways whether we want them to or not. So are you *exactly* the same as you were ten years ago? Physically, certainly not; mentally, highly unlikely. Does it matter? In one sense, probably not – we can accommodate the idea of change within a continuing identity without having to perform too many philosophical gymnastics (although not all philosophers have been able to do so). The fact that I am not the fresh-faced teenager I was 40 years ago is something I manage to live with every day without undue difficulty. However, life may throw up things that are out of the normal. Consider this next problem …

A man wakes up one morning and is convinced he is Napoleon. He has all the memories of Napoleon and no recollection of ever being anyone except Napoleon. How do we decide whether he is Napoleon or not?

Bernard Williams argued that in such cases we have to look for evidence of physical continuity. Clearly on that basis this person is not Napoleon because Napoleon has been physically dead for years. Even if we give significant weight to the man's memories, the only way we can be certain they are authentically those of Napoleon is by assuring ourselves that this man really *is* Napoleon and that there was never a time when he was *not* Napoleon. This can only be done by establishing physical continuity. Without that, the most we can say is that the man has become *like* Napoleon in certain ways. Needless to say, not everyone agrees with this. Would the position Williams takes seem stronger if two people both claimed to be Napoleon?

KEY FIGURE

Bernard Williams (1929–2003)
Most important works: *Problems of the Self, Morality*

Bernard Williams was a leading modern philosopher who taught both in the UK and the USA. His writings were mainly in the field of moral philosophy. For several years he was married to the British politician Shirley Williams.

The Napoleon example may not seem a very plausible one, but a commonly used philosophical technique is stretching an idea to its limits to see if it breaks. On the other hand, disputes and discussions as to whether people are who they say they are are not confined to philosophical discussions. There was a celebrated nineteenth-century legal case in England that hinged on precisely this point. The story of the Tichborne claimant has been the subject of, or has inspired, a number of literary works, at least one film, and even an episode of *The Simpsons* ('The Principal and the Pauper').

Roger Charles Tichborne was born in 1829. In 1854 he boarded a boat bound from Rio de Janeiro to New York. A few days later the boat disappeared, and he with it. He was declared legally dead in

1855. In 1862 his father died, so the estate passed to Roger's younger brother.

Roger's mother refused to believe that he was dead and made enquiries all over the world. In 1865 she received a letter saying that someone claiming to be Roger had turned up in New South Wales. The claimant came to Europe in 1866 and met Roger's mother in 1867. Despite the fact that there was only a limited physical resemblance between the two, and the claimant spoke no French whereas Roger was fluent in that language, Lady Tichborne was convinced that the claimant was her son. After her death in 1868, there was a court case to decide whether or not he was the legal claimant. Eventually it was decided that he was not, he was charged with perjury, and in 1874 sentenced to fourteen years hard labour. He turned out to be someone called Arthur Orton, originally from Wapping.

The main reason Lady Tichborne was prepared to believe that Orton was her son seems to be that she desperately *wanted* it to be the case and could not accept the fact that her son had died. But after thirteen years' absence, Roger would clearly have changed. If he had remained totally unchanged in appearance during that time, like some real-life Dorian Gray, *that* would have been suspicious. It is not that identity prohibits change. We know people *do* change over time. The question is one of degree: how much change is compatible with someone being the same person? ($\rightarrow$ 8) The story of the Tichborne claimant is a real one. The story of the French film *Le Retour de Martin Guerre* is more the stuff of legend. The Hollywood film based on it, *Sommersby*, is pure fiction. But they all pose the same question: is this the same person?

The problem of the ship of Theseus is a dramatic illustration of the same problem. If the ship he ends up with is not the same ship he started with, when does it change from one into the other? After one plank is changed? Two planks? Half of them? All of them? There is no solution to the problem that does not seem arbitrary. We may be able to agree that something has become something else, but it is much harder to agree when it happened.

The ship of Theseus problem is relatively straightforward because it deals with inanimate matter. Recognizing the same person is much more difficult than recognizing the same ship. (→ 6) If Lady Tichborne had lost her boat she might not have been so easily persuaded by the substitute with which she was presented. Many of those who disagree with Bernard Williams do so because they do not believe that physical continuity tells us all, or even perhaps the most important things, about personal identity. Where the parallel between the ship of Theseus and the Tichborne claimant breaks down is that it is easier to agree on what a ship is than it is to agree on what a person is. And while we might be happy to get back a similar ship to the one we lost, getting back a similar person just would not be satisfactory.

In everyday life we expect things to change, but only within certain limits. And different things are expected to change at different speeds. When things change in unexpected ways, we may suddenly realize that the notion of identity is much more complicated than we thought.

The next time you look at yourself in the mirror, ask yourself whether you are the same person you were the last time you looked in the mirror. What would it take for you to answer 'no'? And what difference would it make to you if you thought you had become a new person?

Thou art not what thou wast before
What reason I should be the same?
Sir Robert Aytoun

6. Getting personal

'Person' stands for a thinking intelligent being, that has reason and reflection, and can consider itself as itself, the same thinking thing, in different times and places.

John Locke

In everyday life we are constantly making distinctions, whether we are consciously aware of doing so or not. Some of these distinctions have an important influence on how we treat others. One of the most important of these distinctions is the one between those who are persons and those who are not.

John Locke's attempt to define a person is only one of many. Others have come up with different definitions. Does it matter that there is no agreed definition of the term 'person'? It depends on what use we want to make of the term. Definitions clarify distinctions. To say that something is one kind of thing is also to say that it is *not* another kind of thing. When we use the term 'person' what kind of distinction are we trying to make? Curiously, in philosophy 'persons' are most often distinguished from human beings. (→ 15) This is curious because we normally assume that human beings *are* persons. However, because philosophy requires us to examine our assumptions, the fact that we normally assume something is only the beginning of the matter, not the end of it.

Once we establish a distinction between human beings and persons, two important possibilities arise. First, not all persons may be human beings, and, second, not all human beings may be persons. We will look at the first possibility to begin with.

Can you think of some examples of beings that might be persons but not human beings?

Perhaps the most obvious place to go looking for non-human persons is science fiction. Are the Klingons from *Star Trek* persons? Or R2D2 and C3PO from *Star Wars*? Or HAL from *2001: A Space Odyssey*? Or even the Munchkins from *The Wizard of Oz*? Closer to home, some philosophers would want to argue that there are members of the animal kingdom on Earth that should be regarded as persons, especially amongst the great apes, and many pet owners would make claims for other animals too!

It would be possible to draw up a longer list, but the issue to consider is not so much *who* appears on the list but *why*. One way of approaching the problem is to turn it around and ask 'Why not?' Why should Klingons, for example, not be regarded as persons? They may be ugly, they may be unpleasant and they may be aggressive, but it is relatively easy to find human beings who fulfil some or all of those criteria. Moreover Klingons are clearly intelligent (having mastered space travel), they have a language, and so on.

There are certain physical differences, but are they important? What differences between Klingons and human beings would make it reasonable to say that human beings are persons and Klingons are not? Perhaps the case of HAL is a little easier. HAL is, after all, a computer. In that respect HAL is quite different from the Klingons, who are living creatures. That difference is clear, but is it important? What, if anything, does HAL lack that a person should have?

The rather unsatisfactory answer to these questions is that there is no satisfactory answer. The world does not come delivered to our door wrapped up in tidy definitions. As Friedrich Waismann put it, language has an 'open texture'. A relatively black and white core of meaning tends to be surrounded by a lot of grey where things shade into one another. When the world throws up new things, it is not always easy to see whether we can accommodate them within our existing words and ideas or whether we need to invent new ones. A new car is just another 'car', but if it flew as well, would we want to find a new word for it?

What is important is that, however we use the words we have, we use them consistently. If we apply the term 'person' to human beings because human beings fulfil certain criteria, then we must be prepared to apply the same term to other beings that fulfil those same criteria. If we take Locke's definition at the beginning of this chapter as a starting point, then the first thing to notice is the lack of reference to any physical characteristics. The characteristics he does list seem to boil down to three. First there is some kind of intelligence, which includes the ability to reason. Second, there is some kind of self-consciousness. Third, there is some kind of sense of continuing identity.

Do you agree with Locke's definition of a person? Is there anything you would remove from it? Is there anything you would add?

There is no right or wrong answer here. You might like to compare Locke's definition of a person with this one from *Collins English Dictionary*: 'a being characterized by consciousness, rationality, and a moral sense, and traditionally thought of as consisting of both a body and a mind or soul'. Which do you prefer? Why?

John Locke (1632–1704)
Most important works: *An Essay Concerning Human Understanding, Two Treatises of Civil Government*

One of the greatest of English philosophers, Locke's writings were influential in a number of different areas. Because of his political activities he had to spend several years in exile in the Netherlands.

So far we have looked at the possibility that not all persons are human beings. Now we need to look at the other possibility.

Can you think of any examples of human beings who might not be persons?

Intellectually, this exercise is not particularly difficult. Psychologically it may be. Philosophically we need to be consistent in the application of our definitions but emotionally we may want to come up with all kinds of exceptions. Is a foetus a person? Is a newborn baby a person? Is someone in a persistent vegetative state a person? Is someone in the later stages of Alzheimer's disease a person? The more our definition of a person involves a certain level of intellectual functioning, the harder it is to bring the very young, who have not yet achieved that level, within its remit. And at the other end of the spectrum, it is possible to lose that level of functioning for whatever reason.

While some who argue for the better treatment of animals may do so for sentimental reasons, some argue quite explicitly that some animals have the right (→ 18) to be regarded as persons because not only do they fulfil the relevant criteria but they also fulfil them better than some human beings do. What they argue is that if we are consistent in our application of the criteria, then we have to admit at least some animals into the class of persons and, perhaps, expel some human beings from it.

Does it matter whether someone (or something) is a person or not? That depends on what we think being a person means. The usual point of the philosophical distinction between a person and a human being is that a person enjoys certain rights. We generally believe that persons are entitled to greater respect, greater consideration and better treatment than non-persons are. Persons count for more in the scheme of things; a higher value is attached to them.

To get a sense of what this might mean, we can construct a science fiction scenario where our intrepid heroes encounter three different races. The first, the Admirables, are just like us. The second, the Baddies, are like us, but a lot nastier. The third, the Cattle, are inferior to us in every way. How are our intrepid heroes likely to interact with these three races? Roughly speaking we might expect them to try to make friends (and even breed!) with the Admirables, to be very wary of the Baddies, fighting them if necessary (but with grudging respect), and to treat the Cattle like cattle! The Admirables are treated like persons, the Baddies are treated like not very nice persons, and the Cattle are not treated like persons at all. The point is not so much that we treat the Cattle much worse than the others, the point is that we feel we are *entitled* to. Although 'person' might look like a simple descriptive term, it is a morally-loaded one. We need to be aware of what the words we use mean and what they suggest. ($\rightarrow$ 22)

Human beings generally believe that some things on our planet are more valuable than others, and human beings tend to be at the top of the list of things that are valued. Few human beings would wish to argue that a cockroach was as valuable as a human being. Why not? If the only reason we have for valuing human beings more than cockroaches is because *we* are human beings, that is hardly a very good argument – it is just special pleading. It would be difficult to find a cockroach that would swallow that line! It is the idea of a person that encapsulates what we think is valuable about human beings without having to resort to special pleading. In the science fiction scenario, it was understandable that the Cattle were treated like cattle because they were not persons. Politically, treating persons like cattle is sometimes known as genocide. Domestically, it is more commonly known as abuse.

Immanuel Kant had his own particular way of explaining the special status of persons, which you may find helpful. He said that persons demand our respect, and that we must never treat them merely as objects. We must not treat other persons just as a means to our own ends. I can ask a plumber to fix my leaking pipe, but even though I *use* him as a plumber, I must also *respect* him as a person.

It is not the term 'person' as such that is important, it is the fact that we make a moral distinction between different kinds of being that is important. If we place ourselves on one side of a moral divide, then that has implications for how we perceive the world and how we respond to others in it. The term 'person' is commonly used to refer to those beings that fall on the superior side of the moral divide.

Do you ever treat another human being just as a means to an end?

People are not fallen angels, they are merely people.
D. H. Lawrence.

7. I have my principles

Do to others what you would have them do to you.

Jesus of Nazareth

To say that someone is unprincipled is rarely meant to be a compliment. But what does it mean to have principles? And what principles should we have?

The theme of consistency runs through philosophy in all kinds of ways. For a start, it is the whole basis of logic. (→ 4) Perhaps the greatest philosophical champion of the idea of consistency was Immanuel Kant. When BBC Radio 4's *Today* programme conducted a 'greatest philosopher of all time' poll some years ago, many assumed that it was a waste of time because Kant was bound to win. As it turned out, those who bet on Kant lost their money – the eventual winner was Karl Marx.

Immanuel Kant (1724–1804)

Most important works: *Critique of Pure Reason, Critique of Practical Reason*

Kant rarely left his Prussian home town of Konigsberg, which is now called Kaliningrad (and is now in Russia). Although his books are dense and difficult, personally he was witty and convivial. Even those who radically disagree with him acknowledge his status as one of the greatest philosophers ever to have lived.

Kant was a great champion of what is sometimes called 'The Golden Rule', the idea that we should treat other people the way we would wish to be treated ourselves. He certainly did not invent it, and his arguments for it go well beyond a simple plea to be nice to others. For Kant it was all about consistency. Indeed, the very idea of a rule involves the notion of consistency. Some rules are very local in their application. For example, the rules of football only apply to those who play the game when they are playing it, but everyone playing the game should be equally bound by the rules. The laws of a country (normally) only apply in that country, but they should apply equally to everyone in that country. Kant was more concerned with the kind of rules that apply to everybody, the rules that apply to people not because they are participants in a game or citizens of a country, but because they are persons. (→ 6) To distinguish them from other kinds of rule, I shall call them *principles*.

Kant's fundamental contribution to this area has two parts to it. First, he saw that if we claim to be doing something on principle, it means that we believe we have a good reason for doing it. Secondly, the best possible reason for doing something is that everyone should do it! The question, 'What if everyone did that?' embodies Kant's insight in a concise way. If I claim to be acting on principle then I must be prepared to agree that everyone in a similar situation may, and indeed should, do the same.

In everyday life, we constantly make decisions about what to do, and it would be an unusual person who constantly claimed to be 'acting on principle'. Here are a few things someone might do in an average day:

Have breakfast.
Travel to work.
Do a job.
Watch television.

Which of these do you think involve (or might involve) doing something (or not doing something) 'on principle', and which are done for other reasons? If something is done 'on principle', what is the principle?

This exercise is not as easy as it looks because in each case it is possible to legitimately come up with quite different answers. With regards to having breakfast, it may be something I just do without much thought. I may drink a particular kind of coffee because I happen to like it. On the other hand, I may drink a particular kind of coffee on principle (or at least not drink some other kinds on principle) because I believe in fair trade. I may choose to cycle to work because I enjoy doing so, or I may cycle to work on principle because I am concerned about the carbon emissions and pollution caused by cars. I may regard my job as simply a way of making enough money to live on, or I may have chosen it on principle because it is something I believe in. And when I get home, I may watch television for some undemanding entertainment or I may watch the television news on principle because I believe everyone should be informed about what is going on in the world.

Some basic points emerge from this. First, we can generalize and say that if these four things (and countless others in everyday life) are not done on principle, then we are usually just doing them as a means to an end. I need to drink something, I need to get to work somehow, I need an income, and I need some relaxation. *What* I drink, *how* I travel, *what* I do for a living and *how* I pass my spare time do not really bother me as long as my relevant needs are met. If I prefer to drink organic fairtrade coffee and you prefer to drink the cheapest instant brand, that may be simply a matter of taste and nothing more. If our tastes differ, that is just a (not very interesting) fact about us. However, if I drink my coffee on principle, and your coffee is one that I would *not* drink on principle, then it becomes much more than a matter of taste. And if it is a matter of principle, then the principle should be applicable to others too. If you drink a coffee that I would not drink on principle, then I think you are wrong to do so.

This distinction between a means to an end and matters of principle is a fundamental one in Kant's philosophy and in everyday life. Kant provides us with a way of discovering for ourselves what we do on principle (and so what principles we hold) and what we do not. Until we reflect we may be unaware that we treat certain things as principles (and so expect others to respect them too) and certain other things as just matters of taste.

Kant's insight does not just help us achieve greater self-awareness: it also functions as a useful hypocrisy detector in everyday life. The need for consistency is also a demand for honesty and integrity. At its crudest, hypocrisy is the belief that everyone should act in accordance with my principles except me. And as our old family doctor used to say, 'There's a lot of it about.'

While hypocrisy may be associated in the popular imagination with particular professions (a lot of politicians tend to score badly here), we may not be entirely free of it ourselves either.

In order to investigate the problem of hypocrisy we need to ask not 'What if everyone did that?' but 'What if that were done to me?' Another of Kant's insights was that if I do something, then that is what I regard as acceptable behaviour. And if I regard it as acceptable behaviour, I can have no complaints if I am on the receiving end of it. Why should I expect other people to behave better than me? In terms of everyday life, what Kant is asking us to do is to practise the art of *empathy*. Empathy requires us to put ourselves in another's shoes and see how things look from there.

This is not a formal exercise, but you might want to consider whether you have ever treated someone else in a way you would not wish to be treated yourself. Be honest! This is about awareness, not about guilt! Do you regret what you did? Or do you think you can justify it?

In all kinds of ways and for all kinds of reasons it is easier to see the faults of others than it is to see our own. Here is another exercise that you may find more comfortable.

The invasion of Iraq was justified by George Bush and Tony Blair on the grounds that Saddam Hussein possessed weapons of mass destruction. Was their justification a good one?

The obvious problem with this justification is that even if Saddam Hussein was sitting on top of a stockpile of weapons of mass destruction, Bush and Blair were sitting on top of bigger stockpiles. If the principle they were acting on was that it is acceptable (or even necessary) to invade countries that have weapons of mass destruction, then, if they were consistent, they would have to agree that the UK and the USA should also be invaded. If they would not agree to this, then they could not have been acting on the basis of that principle.

There is more to life than consistency, as will be seen in due course. (→ 17) However, as a rule of thumb, the Golden Rule is not a bad one to apply in everyday life.

The next time someone does something to you that you do not like, ask yourself: 'If the roles were reversed, would I have done the same?'

It is often easier to fight for principles than to live up to them.

Adlai Stevenson

8. What happens next?

You cannot step twice into the same river; for fresh waters are ever flowing upon you.

Heraclitus of Ephesus

The world is a complicated place to live in because things are unpredictable and constantly changing. And yet, despite that we generally seem to manage. How?

Heraclitus (c. 540–c. 480 BC)
Most important works: only scattered fragments of his writings survive.

He lived in Ephesus, although he and the population of that city seem to have generally taken a dim view of each other. He took pleasure in riddles and was given the nickname 'The Obscure'.

Ever since the earliest days of philosophy, philosophers have struggled with the problem of change. When does change mean that something has ceased to be itself or become something else? (→ 5) This is complicated enough when we are dealing with physical objects. Is a chair without one of its legs still a chair? How about if it loses all of its legs? When do a lot of grains of sand become a pile of sand? And so on. When we are dealing with things that are organic, that develop, it becomes more complicated. How much change can we allow, how much change can we handle? If we cannot step into the same river twice, how can we adjust to a world that is totally new every moment?

The general answer seems to lie in the notion of predictability. But predictability itself is predictably problematic. Here is another old philosophical conundrum …

THINK ABOUT IT

How can you be certain that the Sun will rise tomorrow?

You might choose to say that you are not certain. But you will probably still act as if you *are* certain. (If you knew the Sun was not going to rise tomorrow, what would you do differently today?) If you say you are certain, your reason will almost certainly be that the Sun has risen every day so far, and there is no reason to believe that tomorrow will be any different. This leads us to the problem of induction, a branch of logic. (→ 4)

Anyone who has ever made any kind of investment will probably have seen somewhere in the small print that 'past performance is not a guide to future performance', yet in everyday life we frequently assume that past performance *is* a guide to future performance, and the world would be a very confusing place if it were not so. But when we try to uncover the basis for that assumption and subject it to philosophical scrutiny, we find that it is indeed not as solid as we might wish it to be. Induction is concerned with how we go from the known to the unknown, how we go from our own particular experience to a more general knowledge.

A standard example of the failings of induction is the case of the swan. Until Europeans went to Australia, they believed that all swans were white. They had believed this with good reason, because every swan they had ever encountered was white. However, when they arrived in Australia they discovered that some swans were black. The European belief that all swans were white was not remotely unreasonable. On the contrary, all the evidence available to them until they visited Australia pointed in that direction and so none of the evidence gave any indication to the contrary. But it just so happens that they were wrong.

This is the fundamental problem of induction. When we argue from all known cases to all possible cases, there is a chance that we are wrong, because facts gleaned from *all known* cases can never be enough to guarantee knowledge of *all possible* cases. If a conclusion goes beyond the evidence being used to support it, it is always risky. On the other hand, people who have believed for each and every day of the last few million years that the Sun would rise the next day have found themselves vindicated with each breaking dawn. Induction is not perfect, but it can get you through the day. (→ 24)

Science proceeds inductively. The 'laws of nature' it discovers are the result of observation and the laws seek to capture the general principles that underlie our particular experiences. For example, it is the laws of physics, as developed by scientists such as Newton, Kepler and Einstein, that, amongst other things, make the Sun rising tomorrow a far better than even bet. There are *reasons* for believing the Sun will rise tomorrow, but still, the fruits of induction are never foolproof. If the Sun stubbornly refuses to rise tomorrow then, like the Europeans who discovered the black swan, we will have to go back to the drawing board. It is always logically possible that the sun will not rise tomorrow, however overwhelming the evidence that it will. (→ 9)

As long as induction works, it is good enough to help us through everyday life. It works because we can experience and identify regularities in nature. Planting sunflower seeds produces sunflowers, not cabbages. But what if planting sunflower seeds *did* produce cabbages? Worse than that, what if they produced cabbages one year, roses another, wheat another, and so on? Would it be possible to live in a world where we could never know what the outcome of anything we did might be? A world where everything is totally unpredictable sounds like a nightmare. In fact, it is probably worse than that. A nightmare is something we can at least imagine – we cannot even begin to imagine a world where everything is totally unpredictable.

The laws of nature can only go so far in presenting us with a reasonably stable world to live in. A lot of our interactions are not with things but with other people. Here, too, the notion of predictability has a role to play. Although few, if any, people (in my experience) are totally predictable, we expect people to be predictable within limits. We expect people with reputations for being generous to be generous, not mean. If they suddenly become mean, we are puzzled. When people do not behave as we expect them to, we wonder why. We wonder what is wrong with them. Being the same person is behaving (within limits) the same way, saying (within limits) the same things, responding (within limits) the same way, and so on.

Sometimes, people's behaviour goes well beyond the limits of predictability. The 1957 film *The Three Faces of Eve* was based on the phenomenon of multiple personalities. (The film won Joanne Woodward an Oscar and is well worth seeing.) With multiple personalities there is only one body involved, but more than one individual seems to inhabit it. The extent to which these different personalities are aware of each other varies. Where they are aware of each other, they are often antagonistic towards each other. Different personalities may perform differently in tests, have different handwriting styles and almost always have different memories. In the rare cases in which this phenomenon appears, the treatment generally involves trying to reconcile the personalities with each other, and trying eventually to reunite them.

However, the philosophical question to ask is why what is called multiple personality disorder (or dissociative identity disorder) is seen as a problem. The first and obvious answer is that it is not normal. The follow-up question is obvious: what is normal? Everyday life tells us, if it tells us nothing else, that people are different. Some are more volatile than others, some are more susceptible to mood swings than others, some are more forgetful than others, and so on. To see some differences as problematic is to interpret them in a particular way. And because those of us doing the interpreting are all different, there are bound to be times when we disagree as to which differences are or are not problematic.

The fundamental challenge posed by multiple personality disorder seems to be that some behaviours are so radically at odds with each other that it seems impossible to believe that that they could all emanate from the same individual. It becomes easier to believe that there are multiple personalities behind the different behaviours than that there is a single personality behaving in radically different ways. Our idea of normality is based, at least in part, on expectations of consistency and predictability. But how high or low should those expectations be?

The film Invasion of the Body Snatchers *(original in 1956, remake in 1978) has a very simple plot. Aliens are taking over the bodies of humans. They still look the same, but inside they are different. How would you know if the body of someone close to you had been taken over by an alien? How different would their behaviour have to be?*

In the film(s), the main outward sign of people being aliens is the fact that they are actively helping other aliens to take over more human bodies. Beyond that the differences are more subtle. Some see the original film as a satire on the period when Senator Joseph McCarthy was leading an anti-communist witch hunt in the USA: how could you tell from the outside whether someone was a communist or not? If you get the chance, watch at least one of the films.

The other side of this kind of conundrum can be seen in yet another film, *The Stepford Wives.* The women in question become so predictable, so much like robots, that they barely seem human at all. We may think we want predictability, but how much of it do we *really* want?

The world is constantly changing, and yet we do manage to navigate our way around it reasonably successfully. We do so because we make certain basic assumptions that the future will resemble the past, and that changes will take place within certain limits. (→ 24)

WHAT NEXT?

The next time someone says 'That was unexpected!', ask yourself, 'Why? What was expected?'

You can only predict things after they've happened.

Eugène Ionesco

9. You can't do that!

Some things are up to us and others are not.

Epictetus

There is no point in attempting the impossible, but how do we know what is impossible? Some things that seemed impossible in the past are entirely possible today.

Everyday life presents us with a variety of challenges and a limited time in which to deal with them. Epictetus offers a solid piece of practical advice: do not waste your time on attempting the impossible. But how do we know what is impossible? That is a surprisingly difficult question to answer, and there are different kinds of impossibility.

Epictetus (55–135)
Most important works: *The Discourses, The Handbook.*

Epictetus spent some years as a slave in Rome. After he was freed he set up his own school in Greece. His 'books' are compiled from the notes of one of his students, Arrian.

We can begin with what might be termed absolute or logical impossibility. Something that is absolutely impossible is something that could never happen in this or any other world. In practice, most (all?) of us have direct experience only of this world. However, science fiction offers us an experience, if only an indirect one, of other worlds. But for any form of fiction to make sense to us, it must depict a world that we can at least imagine. Although our imagination is in many ways a vehicle for liberating us from the world of our direct experience, there are limits to it.

Can you think of something that could never exist in any possible world? What makes it impossible?

Something that could never is exist is something that possesses a fundamental contradiction at its very heart. An example (often given in logic books) is that of a round square. Something may be round, or it may be square. It may be round now and square later, or vice-versa, or round as seen from one angle and square as seen from another. But what it cannot be is both round and square when seen from the same angle at the same time. (A contradiction always deals with pairs of things rather than things in isolation.) If a round square cannot exist, then no one can draw one or even imagine one.

However, it can be argued that just because *we* cannot conceive of something existing, that does not mean that it cannot exist. Are the limits of our human imagination also the limits of what is possible in the whole universe? That is an excellent philosophical question, but to try to answer it would take us a long way away from everyday life.

For practical purposes, much of our thinking about impossibility is shaped by science, so we can talk of scientific impossibility as well as logical impossibility. The notion of scientific impossibility is the counterpart of scientific knowledge and the two evolve in tandem. In the words of Arthur C. Clarke, 'When a distinguished but elderly scientist states that something is possible he is almost certainly right. When he states that something is impossible he is very probably wrong.' Scientific impossibility is a very moveable feast, and a whole host of things that were once ceremoniously declared to be impossible are now not only possible but even commonplace. It is sometimes easy to forget that before Roger Bannister ran a mile in under four minutes in 1954, many well-qualified people were convinced that *that* was impossible. Why do scientists say that some things are impossible? Because they do not make sense in terms of how they understand the world. A lot of scientific progress has been the result of people refusing to accept that something is scientifically impossible.

While many may see science as delivering the most solid form of knowledge we have, philosophers tend to take a more sceptical approach towards it. (→ 2) Philosophers of science tell us that scientific theories are in fact only hypotheses, ideas that are put forward as possible explanations, but that must be tested. The way to test a hypothesis is to try to disprove it by looking for evidence against it. If no such evidence is found, the hypothesis may be true, but all that we know for sure is that we have no reason to reject it *yet*. When we find evidence against a hypothesis, then it has been shown to be false.

However, people can, and do, cling to ideas and hypotheses in the face of considerable evidence against them. Sometimes this is because there is no better alternative available. Sometimes it is possible to patch them up and make them work a bit better. Sometimes we are just so attached to them that we take a lot of shifting, whatever the evidence. That is to say, we may be psychologically attached to an idea or hypothesis long after logic has told us to let go of it. But attachment to any idea or hypothesis that presents a distorted view of reality must mean that we are making decisions that are not based on the best possible evidence. Today's accepted scientific theories should be regarded simply as the best that scientists have come up with so far. Scientific impossibility is only provisional – change the theory and the pattern of possibilities changes with it. And if nothing else, the history of science tells us that theories *do* change.

In terms of everyday life, it is not so much absolute or scientific impossibility that matters. What is at issue is what we regard as *practically* impossible, and this is mainly a personal matter. Something may be absolutely possible, and it may be scientifically possible, but what I want to know is whether it is possible *for me*. The fact that others may be able to succeed at something does not mean that I can. Some things that are practically impossible for me are impossible just because of how I am. I know that some people can run a mile in under four minutes, and I know that my own body is incapable of such a thing. On the other hand, some things that are practically impossible for me are impossible because of how the world is around me. As I encounter the world I realize that it resists and opposes me in all kinds of ways. I have to learn what it will and will not let me do.

One of the most famous maxims of philosophy, derived from the ancient Greeks, is 'Know thyself'. It has been interpreted in many different ways, one of which is 'Know your limits!' But how do I learn my limits? One of the great teachers here is experience. If I know that, whether I like it or not, the world's hot things can burn me, sharp things cut me, and hard things bruise me, it is because I have come up against them, and probably still have the odd scar to prove it. So much seems fairly clear.

Other experiences offer more ambiguous lessons, however. If I fail to get a job at an interview, what conclusion am I to draw? That I was attempting the impossible, or that I was attempting the possible in the wrong way? To put the same point differently, just because something seems impossible now does not mean that it will be impossible forever. If the problem at the interview was that I lacked a particular qualification, then I can either give up applying for such positions, or I can go away and try to acquire the qualification. To give up is to accept, or even impose, a limitation on myself that does not need to be there. So some areas of practical impossibility seem to be more negotiable than others.

This leads to a more general point. Our own principles and beliefs can also work to impose limitations on us. To take a simple example, if you strongly believe that theft is wrong, then you rule it out as a solution to any financial problems you may have. For you, it is practically impossible, even though in other ways it is obviously possible. Indeed, it may not even occur to you to consider theft, so your principles may obscure from you options that, physically at least, are well within your capability. This is why it is important to examine your principles and beliefs. If you do so, you may find, to your surprise, that you can no longer justify to yourself principles and beliefs that have been quietly guiding your behaviour for years. The effect is a form of liberation. The impossible suddenly becomes possible. And because miracles are impossible, liberation seems to be miraculous!

Here is something to reflect on. Is there something you once believed to be wrong that you now believe to be right? Would you have done anything different in your life if you had always believed it to be right? Similarly, do you now regret doing something in the past, even though you thought it was right at the time?

Coming to see things differently is part of life. Growing up, being educated and gaining experience are all likely to shape our outlook on the world. Sometimes changes are gradual, sometimes, as with adolescence and mid-life crises, they take place more dramatically and suddenly. When we look back, we look back from where we are, not from where we were.

Epictetus is right to caution us not to attempt the impossible. But figuring out what is and is not possible in everyday life is not as easy as it seems. If we attempt the impossible, we are wasting our time. But if we fail to attempt the possible, we are missing an opportunity in life.

Whenever someone says that something is impossible, ask yourself if it really is. And even if it is now, must it always be?

Skiing is a battle against yourself, always to the frontiers of the impossible.

Jean-Claude Killy

10. I had no choice!

Liberty means responsibility. That is why most men dread it.
George Bernard Shaw

How often in everyday life do we hear people say, 'I had no choice; I had to do it'? When, if ever, are they telling the truth when they say that?

Are we free? And if so, what does that mean? In everyday life and language, 'freedom' is often paired and contrasted with 'captivity'. People who are sent to prison are deprived of their freedom. However, this is not the sense normally attached to the word in philosophical discussion. Philosophy tends to use the word to mean something more profound and fundamental.

Before moving on to the next paragraph, please do this simple exercise: close the book and open it again at this page.

I assume you did not find that exercise too difficult? I assume that no one who attempted it failed to accomplish it (however long it may have taken you to find the right page again!). But if it was so easy, what was the point of the exercise?

The point was to illustrate how mundane, but also how complicated, the issue of freedom is. Assuming you accomplished the exercise, could you have chosen not to do so? On the surface, this seems like a very simple, even trivial, question. Of course you could have chosen not to do so. But how do you know? The obvious way to test this would be to go back to the point in time when you chose to close the book and then choose not to. Unfortunately, unless and until time travel becomes possible, you cannot do this. (→ 11) This fact forms a fundamental obstacle to exploring the issue of freedom experimentally.

A different way of approaching it is via a more subjective route. How did it *feel* when you closed the book and opened it again? Did you feel you did it freely? Or did you feel that you were in some way compelled to do it? Unfortunately, taking this route soon leads to more obstacles. Feelings are far from infallible, as divorce courts and discarded betting slips readily and frequently testify. No one who gives it serious thought really believes that the world becomes a colder place when they have a cold, it just feels that way. Indeed, how things feel is often contrasted with how things really are rather than regarded as evidence of how things really are.

Can you think of some occasions when your feelings proved reliable guides in life? And of some occasions when they proved unreliable? Do unreliable and reliable feelings feel the same? How reliable do you think feelings in general are as a guide to life?

Hunches sometimes work out and not every married couple ends up getting divorced. Are some people's feelings more reliable than others, or are they just luckier? Our emotions can be objects of self-awareness and development just as our principles and beliefs can. To be without feelings is normally seen as a sign of being a psychopath, a term that is rarely used as a compliment!

But if it is difficult to prove that we could have chosen differently, it seems equally difficult to prove that we could not have chosen differently! The problem is, if we cannot know whether we are free or not, how should we live our everyday lives in that state of ignorance? (→ 2) I would like to suggest a pragmatic solution to the problem. I have based it on what is known as 'Pascal's Wager', although Pascal's version of it is concerned with the existence of God, rather than the existence of human freedom.

Blaise Pascal (1623–1662)
Most important works: *Pensées, Provincial Letters*

Pascal was primarily a mathematician and scientist who designed a calculating machine. His philosophical writings mainly concern themselves with matters to do with religion.

My version goes like this …

There are four possible states of affairs:

1. We are free, and believe we are;
2. We are free, and believe we are not;
3. We are not free, and believe we are;
4. We are not free, and believe we are not.

We can immediately set options 3 and 4 to one side. If we are not free, then it does not matter what we believe or try to do. With option 1, we rightly believe we are free and act accordingly, which is fine. The real problem comes with option 2. Here we are free but persuade ourselves that we are not. By doing so we deprive ourselves of the freedom we really have and live our lives as if we have no control over them. This, it seems to me, is the worst of all possible options, and it only occurs if we believe we are not free. No comparable damage is done if we believe we are free and turn out to be wrong. Therefore it is better to believe we are free and act as if we are, even if we are wrong.

Note that this is not a proof of anything. One of the challenges of everyday life is having to make decisions in the absence of certainty. (→ 24) The story of Buridan's ass is an illustration of this. The poor animal died because it found itself halfway between two equally attractive piles of hay and was totally unable to decide which to eat.

Assuming that we have freedom, what does it mean? What difference does it make whether we are free or not? The usual answer is that freedom brings responsibility. What we choose to do, we take responsibility for. The question of freedom of choice is something criminal courts often have to consider, and over the years there have been some very interesting decisions. When people have claimed that, because they were being threatened, they 'had no choice' but to receive stolen goods or commit arson, for example, the courts have sometimes managed to be sympathetic. Here is a more extreme case from 1884.

Three people had been drifting in an open boat on the high seas for twenty days. They had had hardly anything to eat or drink during that time. One of them was close to death. The other two decided to kill him and eat him. Four days later, they were rescued. They were then charged with murder. If you were on the jury, would you have found them guilty or not guilty? Why?

The two accused men were called Dudley and Stephens, and they were found guilty. The court appreciated the terrible situation in which they found themselves, but decided that they still had a choice. The choice was literally a matter of life and death; the choice between taking the life of another or sacrificing one's own life. The court's verdict was harsh but logical. Just because one of the options available is completely unappealing does not make it any less of an option. And, as one of the judges pointed out, there are occasions when people are actually expected to sacrifice their own lives for those of others.

It is worth pointing out that what is unappealing to one person may not be equally unappealing to another. That the courts had some sympathy for Dudley and Stephens is shown by the fact that their death sentences were commuted to six months imprisonment. But what if they had been practising cannibals who enjoyed eating human flesh?

To say 'I had no choice' is also to say 'I am not responsible for what I did, because things could not have been otherwise.' To say 'I had no choice' when I know I had options to choose from is to hide from responsibility. As Existentialists such as Jean-Paul Sartre have observed, freedom is not always welcome because it brings responsibility, and that is not always comfortable. It is sometimes easier to pretend that we are not free than face up to the responsibility we have.

KEY FIGURE

Jean-Paul Sartre (1905–1980)
Most important works: *Being and Nothingness, Existentialism and Humanism*

Sartre spent most of his life in Paris and was active in the French resistance during the Second World War. A novelist as well as a philosopher, he was awarded the Nobel Prize for literature in 1964, but turned it down.

Responsibility does not have to be frightening. Often we are eager to take the credit for things we have done, and are extremely proud to associate ourselves with them. This kind of desire for responsibility can even lead people to claim it for things they have not done! People tend to be less enthusiastic about taking responsibility when it may bring with it *blame*. As blame is a form of moral criticism, and sometimes brings with it punishment as well as censure, it is not surprising that people often wish to avoid it.

If I strike someone with the proverbial blunt instrument and that person dies, it seems obvious that I am responsible for the death and should take the blame for it. But is it that obvious? What if I were provoked? What if I were acting in self-defence? What if I believed the other person was about to attack me? What if I believed the other person was the devil? What if I was drunk and had only a hazy idea of what was going on? Clearly I am responsible in the sense that I (in the shape of my physical body) struck the fatal blow, but after that everything becomes much less clear. In fact, English courts have found people not guilty of murder because of all of the reasons just listed at one time or another.

And that is not all. I may have chosen to do something, but have I chosen to be me? (→ 15) Issues of responsibility and blame are not simple matters of fact – they are much more complicated than that.

In the end, if you hide from blame you hide from responsibility. And if you hide from responsibility you hide from freedom. And if you hide from freedom you make yourself a prisoner.

The next time you find yourself tempted to say 'I had no choice', stop. Think: did you really have no choice? Or are you just trying to avoid responsibility?

Man is condemned to be free.

Jean-Paul Sartre

11. Is that the time?

What, then, is time? If no one asks me, I know what it is. If I wish to explain it to him who asks me, I do not know.

Augustine of Hippo

How often do we look at our watches or clocks or ask someone what time it is? Time is constantly in the background regulating our everyday lives. But what is time? And should we really be slaves to it?

One of the things that philosophy does is make us think about things we never normally think about. By doing so we come to learn that many things that seem straightforward turn out to be anything but. In everyday life, time just seems to be something that is there. But there is more to it than that.

First of all, it is worth pointing out that we make a number of assumptions about how time works on a daily basis. When I go to bed at night, I assume I will be waking up the next morning rather than the previous one. (→ 8) We assume that time has a particular direction to it, and that that direction is captured by the combined notions of past, present and future. Because of this, we assume that we can influence the future in a way in which we cannot influence the past. So far, going back to the past remains the realm of science fiction, and most scientists doubt whether it could ever become 'science fact'. (→ 9) We also assume that we can know things about the past and present in a way we cannot know things about the future. The past is fixed but the future has yet to happen, although recent experiments with neutrinos that apparently travel faster than the speed of light may prompt some rethinking of old certainties.

However, different cultures have different views about how time works and not all of them think or talk about it in the same way that we do. Some measure it meticulously, whether in fractions of a second or in thousands of years, others approach it with a much broader brush. Some believe that history has a starting point and a finishing point and that it moves in a straight line between them. Others believe it moves in circles.

Amongst those who believe that time travels in a straight line, some think that the past was better than the future and some that the future will be better than the past. Those who think the past was better tend to look back to a golden age, a paradise lost. Those who think the future will be better believe in the power of progress. 'Past' and 'future' may be evaluations as well as descriptions. There are all kinds of different ways in which we can think about time.

One of the first Greek philosophers to pose some serious questions about the nature of time was Zeno of Elea. He devised a number of puzzles that can still make us scratch our heads. One of the most famous ones is known as 'The Racecourse'. See what you make of it.

In order to cover the distance from one end of the racecourse to the other, you first have to cover half of the distance. And in order to cover half of the distance you first have to cover a quarter of the distance, and so on and so on. But because there are an infinite number of points you have to cover in order to get from one end of the racecourse to the other, you can never do it because you cannot cover an infinite number of points in a finite period of time.

On the face of it the conclusion seems ridiculous. People manage to get from one end of a racecourse to the other all the time. There are two answers to that. The first is yes, of course they do, so Zeno must be wrong. But if so, where is the flaw in his argument? (→ 4) The second is that Zeno's argument is sound, so although we think people are managing to get from one end of a racecourse to another all the time, we must be wrong! The key to solving the problem is this: if it takes four minutes to walk from one end of the racecourse to another, it takes two minutes to walk half of the way across, one minute to walk a quarter of the way across, and so on. All that is fine, but then Zeno changes the rules of the game – he assumes that the distance travelled can be divided into an infinite number of small points, but he does not allow the same thing to be done with the time it takes. This means we end up with it taking a finite time to travel an infinitely small distance. Because there is an infinite number of points in any finite length, if each takes a finite time to traverse, we can never get anywhere.

Zeno of Elea (fifth century BC)

Most important works: only a few fragments of his various books have survived.

Zeno visited Athens with another philosopher, Parmenides, where they both met Socrates. It is said that he was tortured and put to death because he tried to overthrow a tyrant.

Philosophers such as Zeno were concerned with the physical properties of time; with the kind of thing it is. This kind of time is the kind of time we measure with increasingly precise clocks. This kind of time is conceived of as impersonal and something entirely external to us. Not all philosophers have agreed with this idea of time. Immanuel Kant, in particular, argued that time is something we impose on the world. Time is simply part of the way in which our minds interpret the world. We see the world in a particular kind of way because that is how we are equipped to see it. We see the world in terms of certain colours because those are the only colours we are equipped to see. If our minds were set up differently, we would have a different experience of time. It hardly needs to be said that Kant's approach was, and remains, a radical one.

Here is something to think about. If we follow the direction of Kant's line of thought, then if our minds were different, our experience of time would also be different. Assuming at least some animals have minds, and assuming they are different from ours, do they experience time differently?

Obviously there is a lot of assuming going on here! The only honest answer is that we do not know. But the problem can be approached from a different direction. If we discovered that animals do experience time differently from us, would that show that Kant was right?

Even if Kant was right, it does not change how we experience the world, only the explanation of why we experience the world the way we do. But there is another way of looking at time that leads in a rather different direction. If I am bored or waiting for something, time goes slowly. But if I am enjoying something and do not want it to end, time goes quickly. There is a joke (told with many different variations) that says if you give up sex, drugs and rock and roll you do not live longer, it just feels that way. There is a core of insight here: in the end it is our experience of time that is more real to us than anything our watches and clocks tell us.

Finally, time is one of those concepts that is routinely bound up with a number of different metaphors and analogies, and these help to shape the way we think. For example, scientists such as Stephen Hawking talk about an 'arrow of time', while Benjamin Franklin famously observed that 'Time is money.' There is no reason to believe that either of them intended to be taken literally. What Hawking is saying is that there is *a way in which* time can be seen to be like an arrow, and what Franklin is saying is that there is *a way in which* time can be seen to be like money. Time is like an arrow because it moves in one direction, it is like money because it can have an exchange value. Both analogies and metaphors identify similarities between things, but these similarities are only limited. It would be difficult to understand someone who wanted to say that time was like an arrow or money *in all respects*. We would certainly not accept 'arrow' or 'money' as a definition of time. The danger is when we forget that we are using metaphors. Is time something that can literally be saved, as money can? Or is the idea of 'saving time' an unwarranted extension of the analogy that time is in a way like money? If the idea of saving time like money is taking the analogy too far, then it may lead us into unhelpful and unsuccessful ways of thinking. If time is not the kind of thing that can be saved, then it is pointless trying to find ways to save it. Tired clichés may only be tedious and vacuous, but tired analogies and metaphors may lead us up any number of garden paths or down any number of dead ends!

What Augustine realized was that when we actually stop and *think* about time we find that the familiar and commonplace can begin to seem anything but. This is true not only of time, but also of most things we normally take for granted in everyday life.

 WHAT NEXT?

The next time that time seems to be going more slowly or more quickly than usual, ask yourself why that is. Can you make it go more slowly or more quickly than usual?

For tribal man space was the uncontrollable mystery. For technological man it is time that occupies the same role.

Marshall McLuhan

12. How was it for you?

Reality is what I see, not what you see.
Anthony Burgess

While in one sense we all live in the same world, in another sense we all live in different ones. Where we live, when we live, how we are brought up and what we experience can all make a big difference to how we look at things. If we assume everyone looks at things the same way that we do, we are making a big mistake.

Like time (→ 11), reality tends to be one of those things that we take for granted in everyday life. This is a mistake! Far from being a simple matter, it is a remarkably complex one that has occupied the minds of philosophers for centuries. One of the oldest philosophical questions concerns whether the way the world appears to us, to our senses, reflects or amounts to how it really is. There are many different ways in which we know that things are not exactly as they seem. The setting sun does not actually get bigger as it nears the horizon, it just looks that way. A knife does not mysteriously bend itself when it is half-submerged in water, it just looks that way. And so on.

However, interesting as it is, it is not this aspect of the problem of reality that will be considered here. Instead, I want you to think about the extent to which we have a *shared* reality. Do we all live in the same world, or do we live in a number of different and often colliding worlds? When we are dealing with other people, are we also dealing with other worlds? At first sight this idea might seem preposterous. Of course we are all living in the same world! For all of us east is east, west is west and gravity is gravity. That may be true, but it is not physical reality that is the issue here as much as social reality and personal reality.

The idea of social reality may best be approached through the experience of travel. Even moving around our own countries can expose us to different ways of doing things, and this is even more marked when we travel to other countries, especially those where languages other than our own are spoken. In English, 'foreign' not only means 'from another country' but also 'strange' (and the same doubling up of meaning can be found in other languages too). Foreign places are unfamiliar not just because they look different (if they do) but also because people there behave differently. This is easily seen, for example, in when people eat, what people eat and how people eat. The importance of food as a cultural item should not be underestimated, and food clearly plays a major role in everyday life.

The early Cynics, such as Diogenes of Sinope, saw more clearly than most of their contemporaries how much of our everyday lives are governed by convention. That we become socialized into conventions and attached to them does not change the fact that they are conventions; it just makes it harder for us to see that fact.

KEY FIGURE

Diogenes of Sinope (c.410–c.320 BC)

Most important works: a number of writings were attributed to him, but only isolated sayings survive.

Diogenes left his home town under something of a cloud and eventually arrived in Corinth, perhaps as a slave. For several years he is said to have lived there in a barrel.

Social reality is essentially an *agreed* reality. In the UK people agree to drive on one side of the road, in the USA they agree to drive on the other. It does not matter what the convention is as long as everyone shares it. In the case of a convention concerning which side of the road to drive on, the consequences of refusing to be bound by convention could be fatal. In most cases the price of non-conformity is not so high, but legal systems enforce conventions in a formal way, up to and including execution in many places, and traditional practices involving one kind of peer pressure or another do so more informally. Just because something is 'only' a convention does not mean that it is not taken seriously.

Can you think of any social rules or laws that are not *conventions? If they are not conventions, what are they?*

Cynics such as Diogenes distinguished between what was 'natural' and what was 'conventional'. Most social practices they regarded as conventional. Above all they regarded sexual activity as natural, and apparently often scandalized their contemporaries by engaging in such activity in public. It could be argued that laws that prohibit killing are rather stronger than conventions, because a society that did not prohibit people from killing each other would not survive long. If a law is in some way *necessary* that suggests it is more than a mere convention.

While some social conventions, such as which side of the road to drive on, might be formally agreed, many others just evolve. Etiquette is not something that emerges from a recognized negotiation procedure. This is why it can be very difficult to learn, or even be aware of. An outsider might find it very hard to tell what is a matter of etiquette (and so important to get right and conform to) and what is just a matter of personal preference. A knowledge of etiquette may also involve a knowledge of what is to be understood literally and what is not. Stephen Leacock tells the sad story of 'The Awful Fate of Melpomenus Jones' who feels unable to resist his hosts' polite invitations to stay a little longer and ends up dying in their house. He fails to understand that they are only being polite. According to etiquette, some invitations are issued only on the implicit understanding that they are to be turned down.

Because we are shaped by the societies we grow up and live in, personal reality is strongly influenced by social reality. The very language we learn to speak does a great deal to structure the way in which we perceive the world. (→ 22) But beyond this shared reality there is also a personal one, deriving from our own experiences, upbringing, education, and so on. We each absorb and develop our own particular configuration of ideas, assumptions, biases and values. With all these in the background we are constantly interpreting what we perceive, translating the raw materials presented to our senses into how *we* think the world is. This is perfectly normal, but problems may arise if we assume that other people interpret things the same way.

Here is an everyday example of what I mean. When my grandmother was in her seventies she started to become deaf. She would insist that the problem was not that her hearing was getting worse but that other people were speaking less distinctly and more quietly. The basic fact that she was finding it more difficult to hear what people were saying was not in dispute. However, there was more than one interpretation of that fact in play. In her reality, she was not becoming deaf, but in everyone else's reality she was. In her reality, the solution was for other people to speak more clearly and more loudly, in everyone else's reality the solution was for her to get something done about her deafness.

Akira Kurosawa's *Rashomon* is a less everyday but dramatic illustration of the problem of people having different realities. It is also an excellent film. In it, four different people who were there give their accounts of something that happened in a forest. However, the four versions are quite different and it is impossible to reconcile them. They cannot all be accurate. What we have apparently is a clash of four separate realities and no way of telling which is 'more' or 'less' real, apart, perhaps, from what our own assumptions and biases might lead us to believe. There are two obvious questions we can ask about the four versions. First, how reliable are the memories of the four people? Second, what reasons might each of them have to lie? (→ 3)

Just because someone sees things in a particular way does not mean that viewpoint is as valid as any other. For example, we know that colour-blindness exists because we can objectively identify it through tests. We can distinguish between better and worse hearing by means of tests designed to establish which frequencies people can and cannot hear. So we do not have automatically to assign equal value to all personal realities. But I cannot say that mine is better than yours just because it is mine! There must be objective reasons for preferring one to another. The fact that a lot more people subscribe to one rather than another does not make the more popular one better, any more than Chinese is a better language than Vietnamese just because a lot more people speak it.

It is also worth pointing out that whereas we might tend to assume that 'our' reality is relatively stable, people can undergo experiences in life that totally transform the way they see things. Two obvious ones are religious conversion and falling in love. Religious conversion may change our whole outlook on life, whereas falling in love may only change our outlook towards one particular person, but both lead us to see the world, or at least part of it, very differently. How would the world seem to us if we fell in love with all of it?

In everyday life you act in accordance with your own reality and interpret what others do according to that reality. Everyone else is doing exactly the same thing, all the time. So you interpret what I do according to how you see things, while I interpret what you do according to how I see things. Misunderstandings should not surprise us; in fact, the absence of misunderstandings might be regarded as a genuine achievement. Once you become aware that other people live in their own realities and not in yours, you have begun to tackle the reason for many misunderstandings. What you are hearing and what others are trying to tell you are often very different things. Research shows that differences in social class, income and education, amongst other things, can lead to very different outlooks on the world, and the idea that men and women come from different 'planets' is virtually a commonplace.

The next time you find yourself in disagreement with someone, ask yourself: 'Are we seeing things differently? If so, what reason do I have for believing that I am seeing things *better*?'

O wad some Pow'r the giftie gie us
To see oursels as others see us!

Robert Burns

13. There's more to life than shopping!

Money can't buy friends, but you can get a better class of enemy.
Spike Milligan

All over the world, people buy and sell things every day. But over the course of human history opinions have changed concerning what should or should not be sold and what should or should not be bought. It is easy to assume that how things are now is the way things have always been, but that is almost always untrue. If we are to live the examined life we must be prepared to reopen old questions. What should we sell, what should we buy? And, as always, why?

Buying and selling is a part of everyday life for most people. We are not all commodities traders but buying a newspaper or a cup of coffee or a meal is well within our range of experience. Many people are employed in retail or service industries where selling and work are much the same thing. A number of ethical issues arise with regard to buying and selling, particularly related to truth-telling. ($\rightarrow$ 3) However, that is not the topic for discussion here. I want to raise a more fundamental issue. If we enter into a discussion of whether or not it is permissible to tell lies when, for example, selling a house, then we are already taking it for granted that there is nothing problematic about selling a house *as such*. Yet most people would agree that buying and selling human beings is wrong. So we have a sense that it is all right to buy and sell some things but not to buy and sell others. Another way of saying this is that it is permissible to treat some things as commodities, but not others.

Once the existence of a distinction has been established, the question then becomes one of where it is drawn and why. Where is the line to be drawn between things that are commodities and things that are not commodities? There is a further twist to be considered. It may be permissible to buy some things but not to sell them, and it may be permissible to sell some things but not to buy them. All will become clear (I hope) in due course.

History always teaches us lessons if we care to look for them, and one of the biggest lessons it teaches is that things and ideas change. The abolition of slavery is a relatively recent development in human history. Many societies could not have existed without it, and many philosophers were enthusiastic supporters of it. Aristotle took that view that some people were simply slaves by nature, and that was all there was to it. Plato had no problems with slavery either, but was indignant at the idea that people calling themselves philosophers should actually *charge* for their services. Today most people, and especially most philosophers, would disagree with both Aristotle and Plato.

Plato (c.424–c.348 BC)
Most important works: *Republic, Protagoras, Timaeus*

From a wealthy family, he was the most famous and most important pupil of Socrates. He dabbled in politics in Sicily for a while, but without much success.

Can you think of one thing that cannot *be bought?*

A clue to finding something that cannot be bought appears at the beginning of this chapter. Spike Milligan did not invent the idea that 'money can't buy friends', neither were The Beatles the first to discover that 'money can't buy me love'. But if these statements are right, why are they right? The thinking behind both observations is that becoming friends with someone or falling in love with someone is something that *happens* to us rather than something we can *choose* to happen. Can I make myself like or love someone? If not, then the addition of money to the equation can make no difference. On the other hand, the title of Dale Carnegie's bestselling book, *How to Win Friends and Influence People*, suggests that not everyone agrees with this view of friendship. Or perhaps they just have a different view of what 'friendship' is? Whether or not friendship and love are things that can be bought, the fundamental idea remains intact: if something cannot be made to happen, then money cannot make it happen.

Amongst the many things that *can* be bought, there are several that many people think *should not* be bought. The reasons for these views are not always clear, and when they are clear they are not always coherent. We tend to have a lot of opinions without necessarily knowing why we have them or where they have come from. Most people now would agree that slavery is wrong, just as most people used to agree that it was right. But why is it wrong? I believe the best argument is based on the value of, and respect due to, persons (→ 6), but others might have different ideas. The same approach might be taken with regard to prostitution. If a person is treated merely as an object, simply as a means to our own ends, then that person is not being properly respected. But we often tend to think that things are wrong (or right) without having the supporting argument to back up the opinion.

There is a widely-held opinion that the buying of certain kinds of drug is wrong. In the UK, at least, the very word 'drug' tends to be interpreted to mean something that it is wrong to buy, even though there are all kinds of drug that most people are entirely comfortable with. Compare the normal sense attached to 'on drugs' to the normal sense attached to 'on medication'! (→ 22) However, research shows that in some countries the belief that taking certain drugs is somehow wrong has sometimes only emerged after those drugs have been made illegal. It often comes as a shock to people to discover that Sigmund Freud not only took cocaine, but also recommended it. The idea that drugs should not be bought or taken because they are harmful often turns out to be a rationalisation rather than a reason. The damage done by alcohol and tobacco is often conveniently forgotten. (→ 7)

If it is wrong to buy something, then it would make sense to believe that it also wrong to sell it. However, it does not always work out that way. In some countries it is not illegal to buy certain drugs, but it is illegal to sell or possess them. In some countries prostitution may or may not be illegal depending on which side of the transaction you are on. Laws are not always rational.

Leaving aside the cases that have already been considered (people, sex, drugs), can you think of anything that should not be sold? Why do you think it should not be sold?

The obvious way to approach this question is through the notion of a necessity. Would it be acceptable for a government or company to monopolize air and sell it to people? I assume most people will say 'no', and if pushed to give a reason will say that it is because we need air to breathe and we need to breathe to live. If we had to be able to afford to buy air in order to live, it is likely that millions would die. But if that is true for air, what about water? And if it is true about water, what about health care? And if it is true about health care what about housing? And so on. If we are to be consistent, then whatever argument we think holds good for air should also hold good for other things like air. If the argument concerning air is based on the idea that it is necessary for life, then the same argument should hold good for all necessities. Note that if someone is selling water that does not necessarily make it wrong to buy it. The relationship between buyer and seller, both commercially and morally, is often an asymmetrical one.

In the film *Trading Places* (in which a lot of buying and selling takes place), two rich brothers make a bet that has a massive effect on the lives of two other people, one of whom loses all he has. When it is revealed that the bet is only for a dollar it comes as a shock. But would the rich brothers' actions have been any more excusable if the bet had been bigger? Is a contract killer who only charges £50 to murder someone more immoral than one who charges £5,000, or just a lot cheaper?

Something is a commodity if its value can be converted into something else, and as often as not that thing is money. To treat something as a commodity is to set it adrift on the seas of market forces. If we are simply accustomed to treating certain things as commodities and some things not as commodities, we may not be aware of why we treat them differently, and what difference it makes. Becoming aware of the judgements we make without thinking is the first step to taking control of them. One way of becoming aware of what we believe is by reflecting on what we do. Every time I buy or sell something, I am showing that I believe it is permissible to do so.

The next time you buy something, ask yourself, 'Is there any reason why I should not buy this?'

I play the sort of character who would sell his grandmother for career advancement, something
I've come across a lot with actors.

Hugh Grant

14. What does it mean?

Indeed it is well said, 'in every object there is inexhaustible meaning; the eyes see in it what the eye brings means of seeing'.

Thomas Carlyle

We live in a world full of meanings. We are constantly both receiving and transmitting messages loaded with meaning. Often, however, we only have very limited conscious awareness of the content of these messages. The more consciously aware we become, the greater control we have over the process of communication.

There are various kinds of meaning. There is 'the meaning of life', by which we mean the *point* of life. There is the kind of meaning of words that we can look up in a dictionary. (→ 22) There is also the sense in which we talk of things meaning something to us, when they are important to us. What I want to look at here is the meaning of *things*. The world around us is full of things with meaning. Sometimes we are aware of this, especially when we have had to make a conscious effort to learn those meanings. If I learn to drive a car, I have to learn what different road signs mean: this one means I must not park here, this one means there is a low bridge ahead, this one means the road is a dead end, and so on. Sometimes the meaning is obvious and sometimes it is not. If it is not, it takes more of a conscious effort to learn it. Often, we learn the meanings of things without making any conscious effort to do so. We just acquire them along life's way, and we may forget that we ever learnt them. If we do that, it becomes easy to believe that the meanings are actually *in* things.

An example will help to illustrate – what does the flag of the USA, the stars and stripes, mean?

On one level it means nothing. It is just a pattern of shapes and colours. A person seeing such a pattern for the first time would see no meaning in it at all. On another level, it represents the thirteen original states of the USA (in the stripes) and the 50 present states of the USA (in the stars). This can be explained to and understood by anyone. After that, things get more complicated. If you are an American, it will mean one thing to you. If you are not American but have pro-American views, it will mean something else. If you are not American but have anti-American views, it will mean something else again. Each type of person will associate something different with the stars and stripes. It may not be easy, or even possible, to say exactly what it means to anyone. Patriotism? Aspiration? Aggression? However, it can be safely assumed that the flag means something different to someone who salutes it from what it means to someone who burns it. But to someone who has never heard of the USA, it remains just a pattern of shapes and colours.

National flags are designed to mean something because they are intended to stand for their respective nations. When we see a national flag we know it is meant to mean something. However, meaning does not always work in such an obvious way.

Advertising is an excellent example of this. If an advertisement said that if you smoke this cigarette you will be incredibly cool, or if you consume bottles of this drink you will have an amazing social life, or if you use this deodorant other people will be throwing themselves at you, you would not believe it, because it would obviously not be true. However, if you see a poster or television advertisement that suggests these things by putting together two images (product and promise) and allowing you to make the connection between them, you may well somehow *feel* that what is being suggested is true. If something 'speaks' to us indirectly it can sometimes bypass conscious barriers that we put up against a more direct approach. No one ever accused the advertising industry of being honest! No wonder Vance Packard's classic book about the advertising industry was called *The Hidden Persuaders*.

Another way of saying that something has a meaning is to say that it *stands for* something; that it is a sign of some kind. The general study of signs is known as 'semiology'. Semiology is not half of an '-ology': the 'semi-' bit comes from a Greek word, *semeion*, meaning 'a sign', not the Latin *semi* meaning 'half'. All kinds of things, including words, can stand for something, and some of the earliest work in semiology was done in the area of linguistics. Although some philosophers have taken an interest in it, it has found more enthusiastic followers elsewhere. A major figure in bringing semiology to a wider audience was Roland Barthes.

Roland Barthes (1915–1980)

Most important works: *Elements of Semiology, Mythologies*

Barthes had a wide range of interests and wrote several books on literature. He was particularly interested in the relationship between the reader and the text. He taught courses on semiology in Paris for several years, having previously taught in Romania and Egypt.

In his book *Mythologies*, Barthes provides an analysis of various elements of everyday (French) life that he encountered in one way or another. These varied from a striptease, to a new Citroen, to plastic, to steak and chips! The point he makes over and over again is that these are not just 'things' of one kind or another. They are things that have complex *meanings* of one kind or another. The (French) people who interact with them understand these meanings because they are the products of the same culture. However, Barthes does not just tell people the obvious. He explains to them what they understand but are not aware that they understand. He tells people what they have learnt but have forgotten that they ever learnt.

We do not only receive meanings (consciously or unconsciously), we also transmit them (consciously or unconsciously). One particular area of everyday life in which we send and receive messages is what we wear. In Mao Tse-Tung's China, one of the things that struck visitors most was the fact that almost everyone wore the same style of clothing, most of which was green, and some of which was blue. This was conscious government policy, designed to project an egalitarian image (much in the same way that school uniforms are meant to). Apparently, those who became physically close to the elite could see that the quality of their tailoring was rather superior, which in itself sent out a message about how they viewed their own position in society. Given that we all wear clothes, and, once we get beyond a certain age, choose the clothes we wear, our wardrobes are an interesting repository of meaning.

Go to your wardrobe and see what is inside it. If you saw someone else wearing those clothes, what would you think they were trying to say? Is that the message you are trying to send to other people? Do all your clothes say the same thing? Or do you have different styles of clothes to say different kinds of things on different occasions?

Just because some people spend a lot more money on their clothes than others does not mean that they are sending out more or stronger messages. Expensive clothes send out the message 'I can afford them', but cheap clothes may send out the message 'Clothes are not worth wasting money on.' And we can seek intentionally to uglify as well as beautify ourselves. Traditionally, clothing was often used to project a professional identity (which is why we still speak of fishermen's smocks and butchers' aprons), or a particular social status (we still use the terms 'blue collar' and 'white collar' to make a social distinction). Unless you have ended up with a random collection of clothing donated by others, your clothes do, and are intended to, say something about you.

The meaning of clothes is not a trivial matter. For example, there has been much heated debate in a number of European countries of late over what items of clothing Muslim women should or should not be allowed to wear. This is not a discussion about fashion, but about what certain items of clothing (in particular a headscarf and a veil) mean. And because clothes say things, they can also lie. (→ 3) I can put on certain clothes to pretend I am a particular kind of person, or take them off to pretend that I am not.

Signs form a 'known code' that permits and aids communication. If we knowingly choose to send a sign according to such a code, we can scarcely complain if someone else receives it. On the other hand, if we visit India and see a swastika there, we should not read it as an endorsement of Nazism, but rather as a traditional symbol for good luck. If we do not understand the *local* known code, we may misunderstand much of what we see, and in return be misunderstood. There is a close connection between signs and conventions. (→ 12) In the end, signs only have meaning because people agree that they do, which means that only those who have learnt them and know them can use them properly.

As in so many other areas of everyday life, increased awareness pays dividends. While we cannot control the meanings other people read into what we say or do, we can control the meanings we read into what others say and do. The more aware we are of how advertising works, the less likely we are to be taken in by it. The more aware we are of how signs work, the better able we are to communicate the meanings we want in the codes available.

The next time you see an advertisement in a newspaper or magazine, take the time to look at it properly. What is it trying to make you think or do? How is it trying to do that? Once you can see what it is trying to do, and how, you are in control.

We had the experience but missed the meaning.

T. S. Eliot

15. Who are you?

There is in human nature generally more of the fool than of the wise.
                                          Francis Bacon

People often talk about 'human nature', but what is it? What do we all have in common? What makes us different from other animals on the planet? What can we excuse as just being 'down to nature'?

The problem of human nature is different from the problem of persons. (→ 6) Some persons might not be human beings, and some human beings might not be persons. Because we are human beings ourselves, we are in the position of being able to consider human nature from two different perspectives. We can either look at ourselves, or we can look at others. It might be thought that the results would be the same either way, but that is not necessarily the case.

The words 'Know thyself!' were inscribed on the wall of the famous temple of Apollo at Delphi, and became almost the motto of ancient philosophers. The unexamined life that Socrates said was not worth living was the life lacking in self-knowledge. Many of the world's spiritual traditions also embody a call to self-knowledge.

Here is an exercise based on the teachings of Ramana Maharshi, a famous holy man and teacher who lived in southern India. Ask yourself, 'Who am I?' Are you your body or do you have a body? Are you your senses or do you have senses? Are you your feelings or do you have feelings? Are you your thoughts or do you have thoughts? What could you lose and still be you? You can put as many items on the list as you wish. Reject any item with which you do not identify yourself. What is left? The aim of the exercise is to come to see what you are not. *What is left (if anything!) is what you are.*

What we find in the search for self-knowledge rather depends on where we look and how. When the oracle at Delphi adjudged Socrates to be the wisest man alive, he decided that it must be because, unlike other people he encountered, he knew how little he really knew. The kind of self-examination that Socrates carried out was above all one that focused on knowledge. According to this approach, what is required is a testing of one's beliefs, ideas, assumptions and theories.

Not all philosophers have chosen the same route. A radically different approach was taken by David Hume. In his *Treatise of Human Nature*, he interpreted self-knowledge to mean knowledge of the self. The problem was that he could not find any 'self' to have knowledge of. All he could find was 'a bundle or collection of different perceptions, which succeed each other with an inconceivable rapidity, and are in a perpetual flux and movement'.

Hume's observation bears a remarkable resemblance to a central tenet of Buddhism. If there is no such thing as a permanent 'self', then self-knowledge is knowledge of that fact. If this is true, then it must have a significant impact on how we live our everyday lives. What happens to 'self-interest' if there is no self to have an interest? (→ 20)

KEY F⦿GURE

David Hume (1711–1776)
Most important works: *Enquiry Concerning the Human Understanding, Enquiry Concerning the Principles of Morals*

Although now regarded as one of the greatest of all British philosophers, in his own time Hume was better known as an historian. St David's Street in Edinburgh's New Town was named after him and his impressive tomb is on nearby Calton Hill.

An interest in self-knowledge is not the sole prerogative of philosophers. Seeking to know oneself is an exercise that can follow many different paths. The need to pursue self-knowledge is based on the assumption that we do not already know all we need to know about ourselves. That is also the assumption that underlies many different kinds of psychotherapy. The reason why people like Sigmund Freud and Carl Jung became interested in the study of dreams is that they saw them as a source of self-knowledge. In dreams our subconscious minds may reveal things to us that our conscious minds deny. What the work of Freud, Jung and others indicates is that we may not be able to arrive at full self-knowledge unaided. We may need others to help us see what and who we are.

A very different approach again is taken by Existentialist philosophers like Jean-Paul Sartre, who reject the very idea that there is such a thing as 'human nature'. According to Sartre, we do not need to *discover* who we are because we are who we *choose* to be. To deny this fact is to hide from our own freedom. (→ 10) Each individual creates his or her own nature through making certain choices, and what we can make, we can also change. If this is true, it again has a significant impact on how we live our everyday lives. Clearly there are some aspects of my life that I cannot change through a simple act of choosing. I cannot become taller, more handsome or younger just by wishing it. But given the body I have, I can choose the kind of life I want to live with it, and choose what kind of individual I want to inhabit it. How much of what you are do you think you could change if you really wanted to?

So far in this chapter I have been looking at the problem of human nature from the inside, but we can also explore it from the outside. The everyday world around us is full of others with whom we can and do interact in a variety of ways. How we interact with others very much depends on what we think others are like.

Do you think human beings are naturally good or naturally bad or naturally neither?

This is clearly a very broad question, but it is one that has exercised human minds for a long time. How much of what we are is nature and how much is nurture? And of the part that is nature, how much is good and how much is bad? Theories of society in general and education in particular are strongly coloured by our attitudes towards these basic questions. Do people naturally live harmoniously together, or are they constantly trying to harm each other? Are children little angels who need to be set free or are they little devils who need to be locked up? These two approaches, optimistic and pessimistic, positive and negative, run like veins through the history of philosophical thought.

In terms of everyday life, the optimistic and pessimistic views of human nature clearly lead us in different directions. The more positive and optimistic a view we have, the more we are inclined to see others as potential allies who should be embraced and can be trusted. The more negative and pessimistic a view we have, the more we are inclined to see others as potential enemies who should be kept at a distance and treated with caution. So how do we decide which view to take? How do we examine them?

A fundamental problem with examining a basic view we have of the world is that the view itself colours how we see the world. (→ 24) Both the optimist and the pessimist will tend to see evidence that backs up their view and not see, or find an excuse for, evidence that seems to undermine it. A happy person tends to live in a happy world and a miserable person tends to live in a miserable one. The happy person is proven right to believe that the world is basically a happy place and the miserable person is proven right to believe that the world is basically a miserable one. The glass really is half full and it really is half empty, and it really is both at the same time.

Believing that people are naturally good or naturally bad is not like believing that Glasgow is north of London or that light travels at 186,000 miles per second. Even though we might not be able to do it ourselves, we can conceive of how either belief might be tested. When it comes to human nature being basically good (or bad), it is difficult to see how this might be done. What would count as success in such a test? What would count as failure? Perhaps the basic goodness or badness of human nature is not in human nature itself but in the eye of the beholder? (→ 12) In that case, what is there to stop us seeing the world differently? How would your everyday life change if you took a more positive or negative view of human nature?

As human beings ourselves, human nature ought to be a subject that is not only close to our hearts but also one that we are particularly well-equipped to study. It is certainly not one that philosophers have avoided, but it is also certainly not one on which they speak with anything resembling a single voice. As with a number of areas of everyday life, philosophy is perhaps better at uncovering the problems related to human nature than it is at solving them. But we cannot even begin to tackle problems if we are not aware of them.

The next time you think, or hear someone say, 'Well, it's only human nature', ask yourself, 'Is it?'

If men were angels, no government would be necessary.
If angels were to govern men, neither external nor internal controls on
government would be necessary.

James Madison

16. So what?

Any experience is experience within a context.

Alfred Schutz

It seems obvious that some things are, and some things are not, connected with each other. But is that how things really are or just how we have learnt to see them? How we assess situations often depends on what we think is or is not relevant. But how do we know what is relevant?

Everyday life throws many different problems at us but what we never encounter is a problem in isolation. It is not that problems hunt in packs, but whenever we encounter one we always encounter it within a particular *context*. How we tackle a problem depends to a significant extent on the context within which we locate it.

Here is a simple exercise to begin with.

You normally drive your child to school, but he/she asks you if he/she can walk to school with a friend tomorrow. Which of the following do you consider to be relevant considerations in reaching a decision? Why?

a) The age of your child
b) The age of your child's friend
c) The speed of light
d) The distance of the school from your house
e) The name of the president of the USA
f) The force of gravity.

At first sight, the exercise seems like a simple one. It seems obvious that *a*, *b* and *d* are relevant and the others are not. But why? The simple answer is that if *a*, *b* and/or *d* change, your decision will change. You may consider it appropriate for a child of eight to walk to a school that is half a mile away with a friend who is ten, but inappropriate for a child of five to walk to a school ten miles away with a friend who is six. Certain differences make an impact in a way that other differences do not. However, the speed of light is one of the building blocks of the whole physical universe. If that were different, everything might be different. The force of gravity is what makes walking possible. And if the name of the president of the USA were Thomas Jefferson, we would be living in the early 19th century not the early 21st!

What is evident is that for practical purposes we assume that some things will remain the same. (→ 8, 24) As a result, we direct our attention towards those aspects of the situations we find ourselves in that are likely to change; those that are relatively unstable. Because we do not need to (and could not possibly) pay equal attention to absolutely everything, we routinely screen out whole blocks of reality so that we can focus on those most likely to demand or benefit from our attention. There seems little doubt that for practical purposes most people would agree that as the speed of light is unlikely to change, it does not need to be considered every time we have a problem to deal with. As far as everyday life is concerned, this is entirely reasonable.

In one of the few books ever written on the problem of relevance, Alfred Schutz points out that when we encounter a problem, *we* are part of the context. We each bring a different life history to events, based on our previous experiences. If I was nearly killed by a car once when walking to school as a child, that will almost certainly affect my judgement regarding whether my own child should be allowed to walk to school or not. Others, who have had different life histories, may see things differently. (→ 12)

Can you think of any experiences you have had that have significantly changed the way you think about things? Have any particular events in your life had a major impact on the way you see things?

It is entirely desirable that we should learn lessons from our experiences in life. However, we need to be aware that other people with different life histories may have learnt different lessons. Because there is no one standard life history that everyone experiences, there is no single set of lessons that everyone has learnt.

Alfred Schutz (1899–1959)

Most important works: *The Phenomenology of the Social World, Reflections on the Problem of Relevance*

For much of his working life, Schutz followed a career in banking, pursuing his philosophical interests only in his spare time. His early life was spent in Vienna, before moving to New York in 1939.

One of the most famous short stories of the 20th century begins: 'As Gregor Samsa awoke one morning from uneasy dreams he found himself transformed in his bed into a gigantic insect'. Franz Kafka's *Metamorphosis* can be read in all kinds of ways. The point about it to be noted here is that *when we change, so does our relationship to the world*. The first thing Gregor Samsa discovers is that if you are an insect lying on your back, getting out of bed is by no means an easy matter. Because Gregor Samsa suddenly changes, the world he lives in suddenly becomes unfamiliar to him. The things that can, and cannot, be assumed have changed. What used to work no longer does, and problems that did not exist before now do.

In a way, Gregor Samsa has experienced a liberation. He has been 'forced to be free' because the comfortable thought patterns he once inhabited are no longer appropriate to his lived existence. But this liberation is also frightening, simply because the thought patterns he once inhabited *were* comfortable. All of a sudden *everything* has to be considered. The old filters are no longer appropriate. The old assumptions about what is or is not relevant are no longer applicable.

This shift of perspective, especially when used in a therapeutic context, is sometimes called 'reframing'. When we approach things in a certain way, some things seem relevant and some do not.

Reframing involves us approaching the same things in a different way. The effect can be one of transforming a seemingly impossible situation into one in which we have options, or of bringing the previously invisible out into the open. Something like reframing also lies behind many discoveries, where what was once seen as a problem is now seen as an opportunity, where what was once seen as waste is now seen as something with potential. Reframing changes the patterns of relevance. To give a dramatic example, the Apollo astronauts who landed on the Moon found themselves in a very different context, where earthbound assumptions about the force of gravity were no longer applicable. Travelling to the moon was an exercise in reframing that worked through the transfer of individuals from one physical environment to another. In everyday life, the transfer tends to take place mentally, by trying to *see* things differently.

Much the same idea underlies what is called 'lateral thinking'. Edward de Bono, who has written many books on it, regards it as a form of creativity. Lateral thinking may be regarded as a method (or set of methods) for being creative.

One of the methods de Bono advocates involves the use of random words. If you are stuck with a problem, go to a dictionary and pick a word at random. The introduction of this new element into the equation pushes your thinking about the problem in new directions. New connections may be made that would not have occurred to you before. The random word does not in itself provide a solution to the problem, but it provides the starting point for a fresh way of

approaching things. Give it a try! Think of a problem. And if you do not have a dictionary handy, your random word is 'hippopotamus'!

There is nothing wrong in having certain accustomed ways of thinking about or doing things. They can help us to get through a large part of the day. If I make myself a cup of coffee in the same way every day, there is no problem in that. However, if that way of making a cup of coffee becomes such a habit that I am no longer aware that I am doing it, then perhaps the habit is making the cup of coffee, not me. Or if I become so wedded to the habit that I can no longer conceive of any other way of making a cup of coffee, then the habit is getting in the way of my being aware of other ways. When our way of thinking about things stops being a help and starts being a hindrance, it is time to start doing something about it. Before we can break a habit we have to become aware that we have a habit. By requiring us to reflect, by requiring us to examine the quality of our own thinking, philosophy helps us to arrive at that awareness, and to improve the quality of our thinking about everyday life. If thinking about a problem does not get us anywhere, it may be that it is the thinking that is the problem.

 **WHAT NEXT?**

The next time you think, or hear someone say, 'That's irrelevant', ask yourself, 'Is it? Why?'

Chico: What has a trunk, weighs two thousand pounds and lives in a circus?
Prosecutor: That's irrelevant.
Chico: That's-a right, it's a elephant.
The Marx Brothers, 'Duck Soup'

17. It's just not fair!

From each according to his ability, to each according to his needs!
Karl Marx

Few people experience the world as a fair place in which to live. Thieves frequently prosper and the good often die young. Yet few people openly set out to be unfair in their dealings with others. There is a basic sense, especially keenly felt by children, that life ought to be fair and that we should at least try to be fair. But do we really know what being fair involves?

Philosophy lays a lot of emphasis on the need for consistency. (→ 7) Where there is no pattern or consistency at all, we get randomness, and I think Socrates would certainly have argued that the random life is not worth living. (→ 1) However, there is a difference between consistency and rigidity. When accused of being inconsistent, Mahatma Gandhi replied, 'My aim is not to be consistent with my previous statements on a given question, but to be consistent with the truth as it may present itself to me at a given moment.' We would not applaud judges for being consistent if they always handed down the same sentence irrespective of the seriousness of the crime. And we would certainly not applaud them for being consistent if they always found people guilty irrespective of the strength of the evidence. In everyday life, principles have to be applied, and that means making judgements about when it is appropriate to apply them and how. In everyday life, the requirement to be consistent often amounts to the need to be fair.

Treating people fairly is different from treating people the same. The problem of fairness is closely related to the problem of relevance. (→ 16) Every situation we encounter in life is unique. We have never encountered exactly the same situation in exactly the same place at exactly the same time before. There are *always* differences. However, not every difference is equally important.

You have a son. When he is five years old, you give him £5 pocket money a week. Ten years later you have a daughter. When she is five years old you give her £5 pocket money a week. You are still giving your son £5 pocket money a week. Are you being fair to them?

There are two obvious differences to consider. There is the difference between being a son and being a daughter, and there is the age difference of ten years. What difference do these things make? Sometimes being a daughter rather than a son makes an obvious difference, sometimes it does not. There is usually a strong cultural influence on how the difference between being a son and being a daughter is perceived. If we take as a guide Marx's slogan 'From each according to his ability, to each according to his needs!', it can be asked whether the needs of a son and the needs of a daughter convert into a reason for different levels of pocket money.

And do the needs of a five-year-old and the needs of a fifteen-year-old convert into a reason for different levels of pocket money? The ten years have also probably made a difference to the value of the £5. Giving someone £5 in 2000 is not the same as giving someone £5 in 2010. Just because it is still £5 does not mean that it is worth the same. The five-year-old daughter who receives £5 in 2010 is getting significantly less than the five-year-old son who received £5 in 2000. The higher the rate of inflation during the intervening ten years, the rawer the deal.

Children tend to be highly sensitive to real or imagined acts of unfairness, but they tend to confuse being treated differently with being treated unfairly. Sometimes the two are the same, sometimes they are not. Adults can also be guilty of the same confusion. What is a treat for one child may be a punishment for another.

Issues of fairness are not restricted to the domestic context. When they crop up in the public domain they often appear in the guise of justice. The idea that justice *is* fairness was central to the work of John Rawls.

KEY FIGURE

John Rawls (1921–2002)
Most important works: *A Theory of Justice, Political Liberalism*

Rawls' university education was disrupted by the Second World War and he saw active service in the South Pacific. He is widely regarded as one of the most important political philosophers of the 20th century.

In order to arrive at a clear sense of what the just or fair society might look like, Rawls designed a thought experiment. Here it is for you to try yourself.

Imagine that a group of people are meeting to draw up the basic principles of a society of which they will all be members. However, they know nothing whatsoever concerning the positions they will individually occupy in that society. Which basic principles are they likely to come up with?

The distinctive feature of the thought experiment is that no one knows which role they will have in the society they are planning. Because of this, no one can know which principles will particularly benefit or disadvantage them. Potentially, any one of the planners could occupy the worst place in the new society. Under those circumstances, the claim is that no one is likely to agree to a set of principles that would allow the poorest in a society to starve to death, if they could end up being in that position themselves. No one is likely to agree to a set of principles that would allow the lowest ranks in a society to be treated appallingly if they could end up occupying those ranks themselves. This means that the people are likely to agree on a set of principles that guarantee certain basic rights (→ 18) and a minimum standard of living for everyone.

Needless to say, not everyone agrees with the conclusions Rawls arrived at! However, although the way he constructed his thought experiment is original, his conclusions can be seen as a variation on the Golden Rule. (→ 7) If I would find living on the lowest rung of society intolerable, then I should not expect anyone else to tolerate it either. If I would find it unacceptable to be treated appallingly, I cannot endorse principles that allow other people to be treated appallingly. Followed in one direction, this line of thinking leads to the ideal of a society where everyone is equal.

In everyday life, justice and the legal system are often associated with each other, although their association is often a very imperfect one. A particularly contentious issue, and one that regularly makes its presence felt in the media, is sentencing. If someone is found guilty of a crime, what is a *fair* and *just* sentence? In Gilbert and Sullivan's *The Mikado*, the Mikado himself has an 'object all sublime' which is 'To let the punishment fit the crime.' To that end he designs some ingenious punishments tailor-made to fit particular crimes. The crime of being a bore is punished by having 'to hear sermons / From mystical Germans / Who preach from ten till four'! Less imaginative judicial systems tend to limit themselves, in the majority of cases, to imprisonment or fines. But how long a period of imprisonment is appropriate, or how big a fine? It comes as no surprise that the victims of crimes tend to find punishments too lenient, while those on the receiving end of the same punishments often find them too severe.

Imagine you are a judge, and imagine the only two sentences you have available to you are imprisonment or a fine. Which sentence would you give for (a) murder, (b) burglary, (c) illegal parking? When you have decided which *sentence, consider which factors would*

make you give a longer or shorter term of imprisonment or a higher or a lower fine.

There is no correct answer to this. The point of the exercise is to get you to become aware of your own thinking on this subject. When is a fine appropriate and when is it not? I suspect most people would choose imprisonment rather than a fine for murder, and a fine rather than imprisonment for illegal parking, but why? And what makes a crime more or less bad? The amount of harm done? The extent to which it is premeditated? The number of times it has already been committed? It used to be said of a magistrate that she imposed higher fines on those who parked illegally in one particular part of town, and that was because she lived there! Having a reason and having a *good* reason are not the same thing!

In one way or another, concerns about justice and fairness often feature in everyday life. We may encounter them at home, at work or in the media. But although we may have a general sense of what we think is fair or unfair, until we actually put that sense to the test we may not be aware of *why* we think something is or is not fair. Given that few people would probably say that they *want* to be unjust or unfair, this is an area of our thinking that is ripe for examination.

The next time someone says, 'That's not fair!', ask yourself whether they are right. If they are, what would be fair?

Do not do unto others as you would they should do to you. Their tastes may not be the same.

George Bernard Shaw

18. I've got rights!

We hold these truths to be self-evident, that all men are created equal, that they are endowed by their Creator with certain unalienable Rights, that among these are Life, Liberty and the pursuit of Happiness.

American Declaration of Independence

It is difficult to avoid discussions about rights because they seem to crop up all over the place. But what is a right? What does it mean to have a right? And how do we know whether we have one or not?

Rights feature frequently in everyday discussions on a variety of issues. To many (perhaps most) people it seems obvious that we have them, and the only serious questions are how many we have, what they are, and what someone is going to do about them. This is certainly an area of everyday life where philosophy can help to improve our thinking! It can come as a shock to realize that rights, as we know them, are a relatively recent notion. All ideas have a history, but some have longer histories than others.

Here is a simple exercise to begin with. What rights do you think you have? Write them down.

Nothing is ever quite that simple in philosophy! Rights come in a number of different forms. It is customary to distinguish between three basic kinds. Firstly, there are *legal* rights, which are those guaranteed by law. Secondly, there are *moral* rights, which are those we think we ought to have. Thirdly, there are *human* or *natural* rights, which we think we do have just because we are human beings. (→ 6, 15) It is possible for a right to belong to more than one category. Look at your list and see which rights you think fall into which categories.

Whichever rights we have under the law is for the law to decide, and people who live under different legal systems will have different legal rights. Similarly, people with different moralities may have different understandings of what are and are not moral rights. The American Declaration of Independence makes it clear that it is not dealing with either legal or moral rights, but with human or natural rights. Philosophically, these are the most interesting, perhaps because philosophers played a very significant role in inventing them. One of the most important contributors to this process of invention was Thomas Hobbes. However not everyone was impressed by the idea. Jeremy Bentham famously denounced the idea of natural rights as 'nonsense upon stilts'!

KEY FIGURE

Jeremy Bentham (1748–1832)
Most important work: *Introduction to the Principles of Morals and Legislation*

Betham was an active social reformer in many different areas, and an early advocate for animal welfare. He asked to be dissected after his death and for his skeleton to be kept at University College, London. It is still there.

The important point about natural rights is that, whatever they are and however many of them there may be, if they exist then they belong to the individual. If I have ten natural rights and I go from England to France, I take those ten natural rights with me. Thinking in terms of rights means that we are first and foremost thinking about individuals. It is often easier to see what something is if it is contrasted with something else. In order to get a better sense of what rights are and what it means to talk in terms of rights, we can compare the American Declaration of Independence with the Ten Commandments. And to make things simpler I shall focus on just one right, the right to life. This might be regarded as the primary natural right: if you are not alive, the other rights are of little use.

KEY FIGURE

Thomas Hobbes (1588–1679)
Most important work: *Leviathan*

It is said Hobbes was born prematurely when his mother heard that the Spanish Armada was on its way! He spent most of his working life in the service of the Earls of Devonshire. He lived in France for ten years when the political climate in England became too warm for him. For part of his time there he taught mathematics to the future Charles II.

The right to life clearly has its parallel in the commandment 'Thou shalt not kill!' They are both concerned with the preservation of human life, but they approach the issue from opposite ends. The right to life is attached to the potential victim, the instruction not to kill is addressed to the potential killer. If everyone obeys the commandment, then no one is killed. But just because everyone has the right to life does not mean no one is killed. Having a right is all very well, but what does it actually mean? What difference does it actually make?

Hobbes saw this point very clearly and realized that a right was practically useless if there were no mechanism for protecting or enforcing it. To simplify considerably the much more sophisticated argument he puts forward, for individual natural rights to amount to anything, there needs to be some machinery to back them up. For the sake of simplicity we can call this machinery a 'state'. Only when natural rights become legal rights as well do they acquire any practical value.

This may come as a surprising conclusion. The state and the individual are often seen as standing in contrast or opposition to each other. Indeed, rights are often asserted *against* the state. The most authoritative modern statement on human rights, the Universal Declaration of Human Rights adopted by the United Nations in 1948, explicitly includes rights that can *only* be asserted against a state, such as the right to a fair trial and the right to a nationality. But a right cannot be asserted against a state if there is no such thing as a state.

Consider these articles from the Universal Declaration of Human Rights:

Article 5:
No one shall be subjected to torture or to cruel, inhuman or degrading treatment or punishment.

Article 12:
No one shall be subjected to arbitrary interference with his privacy, family, home or correspondence, nor to attacks upon his honour and reputation.

Article 23:
Everyone has the right to work, to free choice of employment, to just and favourable conditions of work and to protection against unemployment.

Article 26:
Everyone has the right to education.

How many of these do you think are 'universal' in practice? If not, why not?

The obvious, and probably correct, answer is that where these rights do not exist in practice it is because states, for whatever reason, have failed to implement and/or enforce them. In practical terms, the argument put forward by Hobbes has a lot to commend it.

One of the lesser known, or certainly less frequently quoted, articles of the Universal Declaration of Human Rights (Article 29) says 'Everyone has duties to the community in which alone the free and full development of his personality is possible.' This is the only place in the whole of the declaration where the idea of a duty occurs. However, a right without some kind of duty attached to it is nothing more than an empty promise. This is partly the point that Hobbes was making (again), but it goes beyond that.

If I have the right to life, that could be interpreted to mean that others have the duty not to kill me. So we could say that 'Thou shalt not kill!' is the 'other half' of the right to life. And if we ask, 'Who has a duty not to kill me?', then the answer is short and simple, 'Everyone.' So far, so good. However, is the right to life the same as the right not to be killed? Does the right to life mean I also have the right to unlimited free medical care, for example? If it does, and we ask, 'Who has a duty to provide me with unlimited free medical care?', then the answer to that question is far from being short and simple. 'No one in particular!' is the obvious, and obviously unsatisfactory, answer that springs to mind.

Why it is unsatisfactory becomes apparent if we think of a right as a kind of claim. If I have a right to something, I have a claim to it. If the right to life means the right not to be killed, then it gives me a claim on everyone. If the right to life gives me the right to unlimited free medical care, where do I make my claim? Who has the duty that matches my right? If it turns out that no one has, then my claim turns out to be worthless.

There is no harm in talking about rights as long as we know what we are talking about. But, as Socrates amply demonstrated, as a matter of fact people do not always know what they are talking about. (→ 1) Part of the examined life involves taking the trouble to reflect on the words we use and what they mean. When someone tells you that they have a right to something, you might want to follow in the path of Socrates and ask them what they mean by that!

The next time someone (including you) claims to have a right to something, stop and think about it. What kind of right is it? Does it actually exist?

In England, even the poorest of people believe that they have rights; that is very different from what satisfies the poor in other lands.

G. W. F. Hegel

19. Anything goes?

I disapprove of what you say, but I will defend to the death your right to say it.
Voltaire (attributed)

If anything goes, everything is permitted. Even the most tolerant of people would be reluctant to say that absolutely everything is permitted. How long would a society that permitted murder last? But if we are going to establish boundaries between what is and what is not permitted, where are those boundaries to be drawn, and why?

Every person and every society is both tolerant and intolerant. We all tolerate some things and do not tolerate others. Modern liberal democratic societies and their members have generally managed to persuade themselves that they are more tolerant than anyone else. When test cases such as Salman Rushdie's *The Satanic Verses* arise, it is easy to feel that the defenders of free speech are much more tolerant than those who think the author should be killed. That feeling may well be right, but feeling right and being right are not the same thing. That is why philosophy constantly insists that we need to reflect critically on things.

The dramatic statement attributed to Voltaire at the beginning of this chapter encapsulates the spirit of toleration. We do not need to tolerate things we approve of, the test comes when we are confronted with things we do *not* approve of. The way Voltaire expresses it ties the notion of toleration very closely to that of free speech, (→ 18) but we may also be called upon to tolerate things people do or believe. In Voltaire's own time, 'toleration' often specifically meant religious toleration on the part of the state, and it had as its background the relationship between different branches of Christianity.

KEY FIGURE

Voltaire (1694–1778)
Most important works: *Candide, Philosophical Dictionary, Philosophical Letters*

Voltaire's real name was Francois-Marie Arouet. Although he was not a particularly original thinker, he did much to make the works of English philosophers better known in France. He was renowned for his biting wit and was a vigorous campaigner for justice.

Not all states tolerate all religions today, so the issues of Voltaire's time have not disappeared from our own. However, even in societies where religious toleration is no longer a significant issue, political toleration almost certainly is. The limits of political toleration are defined in terms of which political parties or organizations are officially banned in a state. A moment's reflection will reveal that the official position taken on this is unlikely to be supported unanimously. There is no point in banning a party or organization that does not exist or to which no one wishes to belong. Consequently, some people will object to the official position because they belong, or wish to belong, to the banned party or organization.

Which political parties or organizations do you think should be banned? Why?

Different people are likely to come up with different suggestions based on their own political knowledge and views. However, the same reasons for banning political parties and organizations tend to crop up time and again. Groups of whatever size or complexion that seek to destroy the state, that hold views fundamentally incompatible with those of the state, or that seek to advance their views through the use of violence are unlikely to be welcomed anywhere.

It is obviously possible to suggest that *any* political party or organization should be banned for *any* reason, but philosophy requires that we look for *good* reasons, and that we are consistent in our application of them. (→ 7) If we are approaching this issue from inside a modern liberal society that embraces tolerance, then the threshold for what counts as a good reason here must be set very high. Organizations that practise violence pose a threat to the physical well-being of the people a state is meant to protect, so it is scarcely surprising if such organizations are given short shrift. When we come to words, however, when nothing worse than preaching is involved, things get more complicated.

The prevention of free expression, usually but not necessarily in words, comes under the general heading of censorship, and censorship may have many targets. While the banning of political parties or organizations may have political ideas as their target, a lot of censorship has a different target altogether, which is sometimes summed up in the word 'obscenity'. A discussion of the one may help to shed some light on the other.

For many years, the working definition of 'obscenity' in English law was something with the tendency 'to deprave and corrupt those whose minds are open to such immoral influences'. The definition was formulated in 1868, in the Victorian age, when depravity and corruption tended to be associated with only one thing! Nearly a century later, an English jury was asked to decide whether *Lady Chatterley's Lover*, a novel by D. H. Lawrence, was obscene. The trial was a memorable one, with many people called to give evidence on the literary merits of the work. The case for the prosecution was probably not helped by the jury being asked to consider whether they would permit their wives or servants to read the book! The case for the defence was probably not harmed by the observation that no one thought the judge, the jury, or any of the solicitors or barristers involved in the trial had become depraved or corrupted through acquaintance with the book, 'It is always someone else; it is never ourselves.'

There is a name for this, and it is *paternalism*. Paternalism is when we seek to control or constrain the lives of others because we assume a kind of superiority over them. In the words of Edna Ferber, and to dispel any illusion that this might be just a male thing, *Mother Knows Best*. However, sometimes mother actually *does* know best, and just because a superiority of some kind is assumed does not mean that it does not exist. While very few people work as professional censors, many parents take decisions on behalf of their children every day concerning what they should or should not see, should or should not hear and should or should not say. At the right time under the right circumstances with the right people, paternalism may well be appropriate. Concerns about fairness ($\rightarrow$ 17) and relevance ($\rightarrow$ 16) may make it not only reasonable but also desirable that we should treat children differently in certain ways.

However, if paternalism is to be justified it must be exercised for a reason. The underlying point made by the defence in the *Lady Chatterley's Lover* trial was that if no one was depraved or corrupted by the book then no harm was done. And if no harm was done, what was the problem?

Increasingly, the focus on censorship has moved from books to other media, and in particular television. Censorship on television is a complex topic because opinions tend to vary according to the time of day something is shown, the ease of access to it, and so on. Here I just want to consider a single aspect of the topic. Do you think scenes of graphic violence should be shown on open access daytime TV? What reasons would you give for your answer?

I have chosen open access daytime TV because many arguments about television censorship revolve around whether children are or are not likely to be watching. In this case, we can assume they are. If they are, why should they not be allowed to watch scenes of graphic violence? The usual reason given is that the experience may be harmful. But harm is a matter of fact and therefore requires evidence. The argument as to whether exposure to violent television programmes or films makes people more violent has been going on for decades, and the best that can be said is that the results of all the research that has been done are inconclusive. People tend to assume that on-screen violence has an effect, but not on them. If on-screen violence would not make an adult more violent, why would it make a child more violent? What is the relevant difference between adults and children here? Does it make a difference whether the programme being watched is fiction or a news programme? Should only non-violent news be shown during the day? To what extent would a news service from which all graphic violence was excluded be presenting an accurate view of the world?

All sorts of censorship aim to deny people access to certain kinds of things. Censorship is usually done for paternalistic reasons in order to protect people from what is being censored. However, the act of censorship may also be an act of hypocrisy, (→ 7) and taken to extremes censorship dissolves into farce. In the wonderful film *Cinema Paradiso* the local Catholic priest previews each film to be screened in the cinema in order to ensure that nothing unsuitable is shown. Every kiss has to be carefully excised. In order to protect the audience from what, exactly? And if the priest could watch the whole film without suffering any negative consequences, why should the people in the audience be any different?

We spend most of our everyday lives acting on the basis of our beliefs. Philosophy invites us to stop and reflect on them. The exercises in this chapter should have helped you to explore the limits of your own tolerance. The point Voltaire made still stands; the only opinions that need to be tolerated are those we do not agree with. And if they have not done us any harm, why do we think they will harm others?

The next time you think that something should not be allowed, stop and ask yourself why. Would any harm be done by allowing it?

The only purpose for which power can be rightfully exercised over any member of a civilized community against his will, is to prevent harm to others.

John Stuart Mill

20. You and me

No man is an island, entire of itself.

John Donne

It is scarcely surprising if we see the world from our own personal perspectives – we see the world from where we are. But just because we have our own view of things does not mean that we have to be selfish. There is nothing wrong with seeking to look after our own interests, but it is not always obvious how to do this. And other people have their own interests too. So how do we decide what is the best thing to do when we are dealing with other people?

Everyday life can be seen as one long, constant process of interaction between ourselves and the world around us. How we perceive that world is a major factor in determining how we respond to it. (→ 12) But any response that comes *from* us is also shaped *by* us. For example, if I see a cat and I am a cat lover, I will respond differently from someone who sees the same cat and is allergic to cats. I will tend to move towards a cat while the other person will tend to move away. But we will *both* be doing what suits us best. We will both be motivated to do what we think is in our own interest. All this seems entirely natural and rational. The idea that we would *never* choose do what suits us best seems ridiculous. But what about the opposite? Do we *always* choose to do what we perceive to be in our own interest? And if we do, where does that leave other people?

The idea that as a matter of fact people always and only act out for reasons of self-interest is not supported by the evidence. It is not difficult to find examples of parents making sacrifices for their children or soldiers making sacrifices for their comrades. However, just because people do things does not mean they have good reasons for doing them. Perhaps people are just making a mistake by deciding to be unselfish?

Here is a well-known problem called 'The Prisoners' Dilemma'. Two men, Bill and Ben, suspected of committing a major crime together, are kept in separate cells. The police only have enough evidence to convict them of a minor crime. In order to get a conviction for the major crime, they need at least one of the men to confess. Unusually, both men have a very good knowledge of the state's sentencing policy! If neither of them confesses to the major crime, they will each get a year in jail for the minor one. If one of them confesses to the major crime, and betrays the other one, the one who confesses will be released while the one who is betrayed will serve twenty years. If both of them confess to the major crime, they will get away with five years each. They cannot communicate with each other. What should Bill and Ben do?

Look at it from Bill's point of view. If he confesses and Ben does not, he will be released immediately. If he confesses and Ben does too, he will go to prison for five years. If he does not confess and Ben does, he will go to prison for twenty years. If he does not confess and neither does Ben, he will go to prison for a year. The worst thing that can happen if he confesses is a five-year sentence, the best thing is that he is released immediately. The worst thing that can happen if he does not confess is a twenty-year sentence, the best thing is that he only does a year. The safest bet for him is to confess, because he cannot assume that Ben will not. And Ben will think the same way. So they will both end up doing five years.

What can be learnt from 'The Prisoners' Dilemma'? It is designed to show that by individually pursuing what they see as their own self-interest, Bill and Ben do not come out of the exercise as well as they might. By taking the self-interested route, they both end up with five-year sentences when they could have got away with only a year each if they had approached the problem differently. However, the dilemma is based on the fact that Bill and Ben are not allowed to communicate with each other. If they could talk to each other they could agree what to do and get away with only a year each. Or could they? That would only work if they could trust each other. Suppose they promise each other that they will not confess. If Bill trusts Ben, then he will not confess and expect to be out of prison in a year. However, if Ben breaks his promise and confesses, Bill ends up in prison for twenty years and Ben is released immediately.

'The Prisoners' Dilemma' originated in the part of applied mathematics known as game theory and is designed to show the benefits of cooperation. Even those who are openly and actively in competition with each other may benefit from cooperation. 'The Prisoner's Dilemma' is not taken from everyday life, but it is not too difficult to think of how its lessons might be learnt there. Imagine a small village where there are two pubs owned by two ex-prisoners called Bill and Ben. For years they have been charging roughly the same prices for everything, and both have managed to make a reasonable living. Now, however, times are a little harder and Bill decides to do something about it, so he lowers the price of his beer by 10 per cent. He gets more customers and his sales go up while Ben's takings go down. So Ben decides to lower the price of *his* beer by 15 per cent. And so on. Before long neither of them is making any money on beer at all. Had they both kept their prices at their original levels, both would have been better off. That is why cartels exist, because they benefit those who belong to them.

Questions about whether we are 'naturally' competitive or cooperative, selfish or unselfish, feed into the broader problem of human nature. (→ 15) They have proved of particular interest to political philosophers. Political philosophers have long asked themselves two different but related questions. First, how did human society come into existence in the first place? Second, given that it did, what is the best way to organize it? One of the ways in which they have explored this is through the idea of the 'state of nature'. Some have thought of this as an actual pre-social phase of human history, some prefer to treat it as a kind of thought experiment.

As a thought experiment, the state of nature is what is left when there is a complete breakdown of law and order. The state of nature comes into being when all that is left of a society is the people who belong to it. What do you think that would be like?

There are two main ways to explore this: imaginatively and historically. A novel such as William Golding's *The Lord of the Flies* is a good example of an imaginative approach to the exercise. It depicts what might happen if a group of children became stranded on a desert island. Historically, scenarios where law and order break down include civil wars and failed states. The break-up of the former Yugoslavia in the 1990s provides a relatively recent example.

In the state of nature we appear as we are when every last layer of civilization has been stripped away from us. Thomas Hobbes famously described life in the state of nature as 'solitary, poor, nasty, brutish and short'. It would be short mainly because there would be little to keep us from killing each other and nothing to prevent us from wanting to. A very different view was taken by Rousseau.

KEY FIGURE

Jean-Jacques Rousseau (1712–1778)
Most important works: *Emile, The Social Contract, Confessions*

Born in Switzerland, Rousseau spent many years in France and some time in exile in England under the protection of David Hume. Some of his writings were regarded as scandalous, and his own private life was not beyond reproach.

Rousseau thought that life in the state of nature was solitary, but that was as far as agreement went with Hobbes. For Rousseau the state of nature was also a state of innocence where the simple life could be lived in peace. Although society might bring with it some benefits, he generally blamed it for all the evils that have befallen mankind. While Hobbes saw the state of nature as something approaching Dante's *Inferno*, for Rousseau it was more like the Garden of Eden.

It is not entirely fair to compare Hobbes and Rousseau because for Hobbes the state of nature was a thought experiment whereas

Rousseau believed it to be an actual period of history. Nevertheless, they present stark alternatives. With very different views of human nature, they were led to believe in very different reasons as to why societies were formed and what the benefits of living in society were. It is difficult to avoid the conclusion that Hobbes' views were influenced by his experiences of the Civil War in England and the period of unrest that preceded it, while Rousseau's were shaped by a childhood spent in rather more peaceful Geneva.

Except for those who turn their backs on the world altogether and become hermits, dealing with other people is an integral part of everyday life. If other people have rights, then I may have duties towards them because they have claims on me. (→ 18) Even if they do not, the Prisoner's Dilemma suggests that working with others may help to deliver what I want. And if I believe that I should never treat other persons merely as an end, (→ 6) that already sets certain minimum standards of behaviour for my dealings with others.

The next time you find yourself in a competitive situation, stop. Ask yourself, 'Is it in my best interests to be competitive? Or would it be better to be cooperative?'

It is not a correct deduction from the Principles of Economics that enlightened self-interest always works in the public interest.
John Maynard Keynes

21. Truth and consequences

Whenever a dispute is serious, we ought to be able to show some practical difference that must follow from one side or the other being right.

William James

What is the use of knowledge? How is it acquired? How do we test it?

The Sceptics may well be right to say that certainty is extremely difficult, or perhaps even impossible, to come by. (→ 2) But even if they are, that does not mean that every piece of uncertainty is as good or as bad as any other. If we seriously believe that a miss is as good as a mile, then we are highly unlikely ever to improve or learn anything. While some mistakes we make in life may indeed be total disasters, at least some of them offer us the chance to learn something. But we can only learn something if we know how to.

In everyday language, 'pragmatism' suggests a lack of concern with theory, but in philosophy pragmatism *is* a theory. It is particularly associated with three American philosophers, Charles Sanders Peirce, John Dewey and William James. They were three interesting characters, all with a wide range of interests. Peirce was influential in the development of semiology, (→ 14) Dewey in the philosophy of education and James in psychology.

Charles Sanders Peirce (1839–1914)

Most important works: he wrote many philosophical essays that appear in a variety of different collections.

Peirce's main career was as a scientist, especially in the areas of astronomy and physics. His main philosophical interests were in logic. He spent the last years of his life in great poverty, supported by a number of friends including William James.

Although Peirce may be regarded as the founder of pragmatism, it was James who did most to bring it to a wider audience. The fundamental principle of pragmatism is that both the value of knowledge and the test for knowledge lie in the practical implications of knowledge. Something is right to the extent that it works. Something is meaningless to the extent that it has no possible practical implications whatsoever.

Here is an exercise based on one that was designed by William James. Many religious people claim that the world was created by God. Many scientific people claim that the world was created by a Big Bang. How do you decide which of them is right?

The conclusion James came to was that it is impossible to decide. We experience the world the same way whether it was created by God or a Big Bang. For present purposes, the question is irrelevant. However, that does not mean that it is wholly meaningless. If we think of the future, of the end of the world, we can see that it might make a difference *then* how the world came into being. If God created it, we might expect the world to end differently from how it would end if it had been created by a Big Bang. If we cannot conceive of any possible difference it could ever make whether God created the world or the Big Bang did, it would be a completely meaningless question. The world is exactly the same place either way.

Part of the programme of the pragmatists was to persuade us to stop wasting our time thinking about things that were not worth thinking about. If there is no answer to a question, or if it does not matter for practical purposes what the answer to the question is, then the question can be ignored or dismissed. In one way or another, everyday life is where our beliefs are tested. It may be a cliché, but the university of life is where we do a lot of our learning. So how should we go about it?

KEY FIGURE

William James (1842–1910)
Most important works: *Pragmatism, Principles of Psychology, The Varieties of Religious Experience*

The brother of the novelist Henry James, despite frequent poor health, William James was widely travelled. His interest in mysticism led him to experiment with the psychoactive properties of certain drugs.

One of the great debates in philosophy over the centuries has been about where knowledge comes from. Are we born with it? Can we develop it by just thinking about things? Or do we derive it from experience? It may be that we get knowledge from all three sources, but some knowledge, at least, seems to rely on experience, on a process of trial and error. We can call this process 'The 3 Rs', which stand for Reflect, Refine Repeat.

Reflecting is a fundamental part of the examined life. In the process of trial and error, reflection involves looking at what went wrong. Or, if nothing actually went *wrong*, looking at what could go *better*. Refining involves working out which changes would deliver an improvement. Repeating puts the changes to the test in order to see if they do what they are meant to do. And then the whole process starts all over again.

A simple illustration shows the process at work. I have moved to a new house and want to walk to work in the shortest possible time. If I am remotely reflective I do not assume that the first route I choose to take is the best one. I may have chosen it because it looks like the shortest one on the map, but then I find I spend a lot of time crossing some busy roads if I go that way, so it may not be the quickest. So I try a number of different routes, and eventually find the one that seems to consistently deliver the best time. The process of reflecting, refining and repeating has paid off. Success!

Some things in everyday life really are that simple. Unfortunately, a lot of other things in everyday life are not. If I want to walk to work in the shortest possible time, I know where I want to get to (work), I know how I want to get there (by walking) and I know what success is (the shortest possible time). Knowing these three things, I can fairly easily achieve success through a process of trial and error. But it is not always that easy. Suppose someone stops you in the street and asks you for the best way to get to a certain shop. You might assume that by 'the best way', they mean the quickest one. However, being a philosopher you know better than to make any unnecessary assumptions, (→ 24) so you ask them what they mean by 'the best way'. If they say they mean the quickest or the shortest way, then you know how to answer them. But if they say, 'I just mean the best way', then you do not know how to answer them because you do not know what they are asking for. (→ 22)

In John Bunyan's *The Pilgrim's Progress*, the hero, Christian, is on a journey. However, we are clearly meant to understand that this is not a physical journey but a spiritual one. Likening life, or some aspect of it, to a journey is neither novel nor profound, but it can sometimes be useful.

This exercise is a very demanding one. There is no right or wrong answer, but it may require a great deal of reflection. If you think of your life as a journey to somewhere, where are you trying to get to?

If I am trying to walk to work and I follow a beautiful route along rivers and through fields but I end up somewhere other than at work, then something has gone wrong. I know that because I do not end up where I want to be. But if I do not know where I want to be, then I do not know whether something has gone wrong or not. Perhaps it does not matter. Perhaps all I want is an enjoyable walk. But in that case *enjoyment* is the aim, and if I do not enjoy it, then something has gone wrong. The process of trial and error only works if we know what an error looks like. If there is no such thing as being wrong, then, equally, there is no such thing as being right. And if there are no errors, then there is nothing to learn from.

Unfortunately, everyday life does not come with an instruction book so we have to learn a lot about it along the way. If we are unable to learn, we are unlikely to make much progress. But unless we know what our mistakes look like we will never learn anything from them. To err is not only human, it is essential!

The next time you make a mistake, ask yourself, 'What can I learn from this?'

I have learnt from my mistakes and I am sure I can repeat them.
Peter Cook (as Sir Arthur Streeb-Greebling)

22. Mind your language!

What can be said at all can be said clearly.
Ludwig Wittgenstein

In everyday life we tend to take language for granted. It is just what we use to communicate with other people. However, it is not that simple. We cannot assume that everything we can say actually makes sense. We cannot assume that every question that can be asked has or needs an answer. In fact, the language that we use can lead us into all kinds of traps if we are not careful.

For much of the twentieth century, philosophy in the English-speaking world was dominated by a concern (some would say an obsession) with language. The presiding genius of this development was undoubtedly Ludwig Wittgenstein, but he had many able and willing supporters and followers. There was a strong belief that philosophers of the past had paid insufficient attention to language and as a result strayed up numerous blind alleys. Philosophers had failed to answer various questions because they had failed to realize that the questions themselves were meaningless.

Ludwig Wittgenstein (1889–1951)

Most important works: *Tractatus Logico-Philosophicus, Philosophical Investigations*

Born into a rich Viennese family, Wittgenstein first came to England to study aeronautics. He served in the Austrian army in World War One and worked as a hospital porter in England in World War Two.

But why should anyone even *try* to answer a question that has no meaning? Because people sometimes think a question does have a meaning when in fact it does not. There is another scenario that is less drastic but perhaps more common. That is when a question has more than one possible meaning and can be interpreted in more than one way. In that case it is not so much one question as several, and a correct answer to one interpretation may not be a correct answer to another. Some examples may help to illustrate the basic point.

Consider this question: 'When did democracy get married?' Does it mean anything? If so, what does it mean? If not, why not?

It is always a bit dangerous to say that something could *never* mean anything. Literature and the visual arts provide many examples of symbolic or allegorical 'weddings' of various kinds, so first we must make it clear that we are looking for a *literal* meaning here. In a literal sense, 'When did democracy get married?' is meaningless because democracy is not the kind of thing that can get married. The question is an example of what G. E. Moore called a 'category mistake'. The question mixes up two different kinds of things, things that can get married and things that cannot get married. So it is pointless to try to decide when democracy got married because democracy can never get married. If we try to answer the 'when' bit of the question without noticing that the rest of the question makes no sense, we are on a wild goose chase.

Unfortunately, things are rarely that easy! Appearances are usually more deceptive. Here is a more difficult example.

Consider this question: 'Is democracy the best form of government?' Does that mean anything? If so, what does it mean? If not, why not?

On the face of it, this question obviously makes sense in a way in which the previous one did not. However, before we can begin to answer it we need to consider whether the sense of the question is clear. What is democracy? Is there an agreed definition? Can you have a democracy without elections? Can you have a democracy without freedom of speech? Can you have a democracy without a welfare state? And so on. The question 'What is democracy?' needs to be answered before we can assess whether democracy is the best form of government, and when we dig into the subject we find that there are many different opinions as to what democracy is. But assuming we can agree on what democracy is, how do we decide whether or not it is the best form of government? Is the best form of government the one that delivers the greatest freedom? The one that delivers the greatest power? The one that delivers the best economic growth? And so on, again. Needless to say, there are many different opinions on this matter as well! The question 'Is democracy the best form of government?' makes sense, but there is a lot of work to be done before we can be clear precisely what the question is asking.

What Wittgenstein and his followers argue is that until a question is clear there is no point in trying to answer it, and if the question cannot be made clear then it is not a real question. The fact that it may look like a real question does not make it one. What is required is a careful analysis of the question in order to identify precisely what it is asking for. And when we have carried out that task, then not only the question but also the answer should be clear.

When Wittgenstein's method is applied to the first example, 'When did democracy get married?', it is obvious that there is no answer to be found because the question itself makes no sense. When it is applied to the second example, the outcome is both different and more complex. The question 'Is democracy the best form of government?' becomes 'Is democracy (by which we mean the form of government with characteristics a, b, and c) the best form of government (by which we mean the form of government that performs best according to criteria x, y and z)?' If we can get the question to this level of clarity, then it should be relatively easy to answer it.

Often, however, we cannot bring the question to this level of clarity. Often it turns out that although *I* think democracy means 'the form of government with characteristics a, b, and c', *you* think it means 'the form of government with characteristics d, e, and f'. And while for *me* the best form of government is the one that performs best in terms of x, y, and z, for *you* it is the one that performs best in terms of 1, 2 and 3! If the same words can be interpreted in different ways, then what looks like one question is in fact several questions. Each different interpretation of 'democracy' gives a different meaning to the question 'Is democracy the best form of government?' If people disagree on the answer to the question, it may be that they are in fact answering different questions. Suppose I ask you the best road to take to Edinburgh. By 'best', I mean 'the most scenic'. Unfortunately, by 'best' you understand 'quickest'. The route you recommend is unlikely to be the one I am looking for.

This approach to philosophy came to be criticized by many for being pedantic and avoiding rather than confronting the more pressing issues of everyday life. Everyday life is not all about language and sometimes the questions are all too clear but the answers remain all too elusive.

However, it was not just philosophers who were concerned about the traps that language can lay for the unwary. One of the best-known novels of the 20th century was published shortly before Wittgenstein died. It was called *Nineteen Eighty-Four*. One of the more alarming aspects of the imaginary society that George Orwell portrays there is its language, Newspeak. 'The purpose of Newspeak was not only to provide a medium of expression for the world-view and mental habits proper to the devotees of Ingsoc [the Newspeak name for 'English Socialism'], but to make all other modes of thought impossible.' A fundamental idea running through *Nineteen Eighty-Four*, as well as through a lot of Orwell's non-fiction, is the connection between language and thought, which operates in two directions: lazy thinking expresses itself in a lazy use of language, and a limited language sets limits to what we can think. As a journalist, Orwell was particularly concerned with the problem of propaganda. In his essay on 'Politics and the English Language' he wrote, 'Political language is designed to make lies sound truthful and murder respectable, and to give an appearance of solidarity to pure wind.'

Outright lies occupy one end of a spectrum that also finds room for spin and 'making the best of a bad job'. Furthermore, while politicians bore the brunt of Orwell's scorn, the media are far from innocent. Consider these two sentences. (a) Our brave boys launched a surprise attack; (b) The cowardly enemy launched a sneak attack. What is the difference between them?

The main difference between them lies not so much in what they say but in how you are expected to respond to them. You are clearly expected to approve of what is described in (a) and disapprove of what is described in (b). You may even identify with those described in (a), but are unlikely to identify with those described in (b). But what is happening in both cases is that one group of people attacks another group of people without announcing the fact in advance.

Encountering this exercise in a book like this alerts you to be on the lookout for what is going on. By becoming aware of the attempt to manipulate you into taking one side against the other, you become able to choose not to be manipulated. Encountering something similar in the media everyday is a very different experience. Unless we are aware that language is being used to manoeuvre us into taking certain sides or forming certain judgements, we are very much at the mercy of the media.

WHAT NEXT?

The next time you read a newspaper story, ask yourself how much it is trying to communicate factual information and how much it is trying to influence your thinking. What is fact and what is opinion? Get into the habit of looking beyond the words to see to what is really going on.

The basic tool for the manipulation of reality is the manipulation of words. If you can control the meaning of words, you can control the people who must use the words.

Philip K. Dick

23. A matter of life and death

It's not that I'm afraid to die. I just don't want to be there when it happens.
Woody Allen

Captain Kirk was wrong: death, not space, is the final frontier. And journeys across that frontier only seem to happen in one direction. To think of nothing but death may be morbid, but to pretend it will never happen is to live in a fool's paradise. In life, death demands our attention.

Whichever way we look at it, death is something we cannot avoid facing in everyday life. Some may manage to avoid taxation, but death remains a certainty. It also remains a great *un*certainty, although there is no shortage of beliefs about it. Different cultures and religions dress it up in a variety of ways because what cannot be avoided must be dealt with.

Philosophers have not flinched from the challenge of dealing with death. Some of them have had very dramatic deaths of their own. Empedocles is said to have ended his life by leaping into the crater of Mount Etna. Socrates carried out his fellow citizens' death sentence upon himself by drinking hemlock. Seneca met his end by slashing his veins, taking poison and suffocating himself. It is not known exactly how Epicurus died, although he had health problems for many years.

KEY FIGURE

Empedocles (fifth century BC)
Most important work: fragments that seem to come from two poems called *On Nature* and *Purifications* survive.

He came from Agrigento in Sicily, and believed that everything was composed of earth, fire, air and water. He believed in human reincarnation, and some thought he possessed magical powers.

Epicurus strongly believed that people were frightened of things mainly because they did not understand them – if things could be explained properly, then a lot of anxieties would just vanish. He recognized that death was one of the things that people were most frightened of and sought to reassure them that they had no reason to feel this. He could not make death go away, but he believed he could help people to put it into the right perspective. He summarized his position as follows, 'Death is nothing to us; since when we exist, death is not yet present, and when death is present, then we do not exist.' His main reason for thinking this was a scientific one. As someone who believed that we are all made up of atoms, Epicurus reasoned that when we die, the atoms just disperse. It is like when the tide comes in and washes a sandcastle away. The sandcastle has not gone anywhere, it has just stopped existing. What was once a sandcastle is now just a lot of sand.

Epicurus (c.340–c.270 BC)
Most important works: he wrote a great deal, but little remains apart from some fragments and a few letters.

Epicurus was born in Samos, but later settled in Athens and founded a philosophical community there called 'The Garden'. He was a scientist as much as a philosopher and believed he had discovered explanations for different kinds of weather.

A very similar approach was taken by Ludwig Wittgenstein, although he based his argument on philosophy rather than science, 'Death is not an event in life: we do not live to experience death.' Death does not happen to *me* because *I* am a living being. By the time death happens, I have already gone. It may seem as if Epicurus and Wittgenstein are just playing with words, but their intentions are entirely serious. If death does not happen to us, because it cannot, there is no need to fear it. It is an event that happens in a world from which I have already departed. If Wittgenstein is right, Woody Allen will get his wish.

Take some time to reflect on your own views on death. Do you think it is the end of everything, or do you think there is some kind of 'life

after death'? Why do you think this? Have your views about death ever changed?

There are no answers to be handed out here, but it may be observed that most people who believe in life after death do so for religious reasons of one kind or another. However, the Dalai Lama once argued that we should believe in it for scientific reasons. The general line of his argument was quite simple: science tells us that energy is neither created nor destroyed. A dead body has considerably less energy than a living one. So where has the missing energy gone?

Some philosophers have argued that death *must* be the end of us, because the alternative does not make any sense. Given that the body is clearly dead, what or where is the 'I' that could still be alive in some way? It is certainly true that as a human being death seems to be the end of things, because our bodies are part of what makes us human beings, and a fairly indispensable part at that! (→ 15) However, if we distinguish between human beings and persons, (→ 6) then unless all and only human beings are persons, it is possible for some things to be true of persons that are not true of human beings. For example, John Locke's definition of a person as 'a thinking intelligent being, that has reason and reflection, and can consider itself as itself, the same thinking thing, in different times and places', makes no mention of a physical body, human or otherwise. However, those who reject the possibility of life after death would argue that only something with a physical body could be the kind of being Locke describes. They do not reject life after death as *scientifically* impossible but as *logically* impossible. (→ 9) According to them the kind of thing that has reason and reflection, etc., cannot also be the kind of thing that has no physical body. If they are right, then any evidence that seems to suggest the possibility of life after death must be rejected. There cannot be any evidence for anything that is logically impossible. The debate goes on.

Dealing with my own death is one thing, dealing with the deaths of others is something different. I only have to deal with my own death once, while the deaths of others may happen all too often. Centuries ago, the Greek historian Herodotus observed that societies take their conventions about death very seriously. He tells the tale of the Persian king, Darius, who put this to the test. He first asked some Greeks at his court whether they would consider eating a dead body. The Greeks were horrified at the suggestion. He then asked some people from India at his court whether they would consider burning a dead body. They were equally horrified at that suggestion. Darius knew, as you may have guessed, that the Greeks burned their dead and the people from India ate theirs. The point of the story was not only to illustrate the difference between the conventions of the two groups of people, but also to show the strength of their attachment to their own conventions. (→ 12)

Such differences are still with us. After her husband, Prince Albert, died in 1861, Queen Victoria wore black clothes in mourning for him for the rest of her life. She died in 1901. I recently attended the funeral of a friend. At the request of his widow, no one wore black. In China, white, not black is the colour of death because white is the colour of ghosts. The outward symbols have their meaning, (→ 14) but the meaning of symbols changes over time. In some ways the ancient Sceptics had the answer: (→ 2) you do what most others do. But there comes a point where those who live the examined life start to feel uncomfortable with what most others do. Why waste time thinking for yourself if you are only going to end up following the herd?

When Princess Diana died in 1997, there was a massive outpouring of grief, mostly from those who had never met her. As with the Greeks and the Indians at the court of Darius, there was a significant difference of opinion over this. Those who joined in the public grief obviously felt that it was appropriate, while those who did not could not understand it.

What did you feel about the public grief when Princess Diana died? Why?

Again, this is a matter for reflection rather than a question that has a right or wrong answer. We do not need to meet people in order for them to occupy an important place in our lives. When Rudolf Valentino died, something similar happened. People felt they had a personal connection with him through watching his films. If there is a genuine and strong connection with someone who dies, then grief is appropriate. The question is then whether the connection is genuine and strong. But if we feel that it is, is that all that is needed? And when does genuine grief become excessive?

The Stoics had a reputation for being the cold fish among ancient philosophers. This was probably deserved. Here is Seneca's advice to someone who has lost a close friend, 'Supposing someone had lost his one and only shirt in a robbery, would you not think him an utter idiot if he chose to bewail his loss rather than look about him for some means of keeping out the cold?' A dead friend is like a lost shirt?

KEY FIGURE

Lucius Annaeus Seneca (4 BC–65 AD)
Most important works: *Moral Essays, Letters*

Originally from Cordoba, Seneca moved to Rome and enjoyed a successful career in public life. Being involved in politics had its risks – although he had been a tutor to Nero before he became emperor, Nero later passed a death sentence on Seneca.

However, if the Stoics took an extreme view, which is the right one? As usual, the questions are easier to ask than to answer. One thing is sure, until such time as immortality is guaranteed for all, death will remain an unavoidable problem to be faced in everyday life.

WHAT NEXT?

If you believed you were going to live forever, how would you live your life differently?

Die, my dear Doctor, that's the last thing I shall do!
Lord Palmerston (attributed last words)

24. Who says?

Without risk there is no faith.

Søren Kierkegaard

Everyday life requires us to do the best we can with the means at our disposal. Because we cannot know everything, we often end up taking things on trust and making a lot of assumptions. There is nothing wrong with making assumptions, as long as we are aware that that is what we are doing. But taking things on trust always involves taking a risk.

Faith assumes many forms in everyday life. The notion of faith is perhaps most commonly encountered in the religious context, and indeed religions are now often *called* 'faiths'. Faith doubtless has a role to play in some or all religions, and finds its most extreme expression in the words of the theologian Tertullian, 'It is certain because it is impossible.' At its extreme, faith may involve believing the apparently unbelievable. However, everyday life routinely involves far less drastic or dramatic demonstrations of faith. In all kinds of ways, faith is what gets a lot of people through the day. Faith may be seen as the counterpart to the ancient form of Scepticism associated with Pyrrho. (→ 2) The Sceptics refused to pass judgement where the evidence was not overwhelming, which meant that they rarely if ever passed judgement at all. Faith, on the other hand, involves choosing to believe something despite the fact that the evidence is not overwhelming. If the evidence were overwhelming, faith would not be needed. Because the evidence is not overwhelming, there is always the chance of being wrong. That is why Kierkegaard saw an obvious connection between risk and faith. Faith is inherently dangerous because it could always be misplaced.

KEY FIGURE

Søren Kierkegaard (1813–1855)
Most important works: *Concluding Unscientific Postscript, The Concept of Dread, Fear and Trembling*

Apart from a short period in Berlin, Kierkegaard spent his entire life in Copenhagen, relieved of the need to work by the money his father had left him. Many of his books were originally published under a variety of pseudonyms to avoid him being identified too closely with the ideas he was putting forward.

Existentialists such as Kierkegaard tend to put great emphasis on the irrationality of faith, as if the observation made by Tertullian was the norm rather than the extreme. In fact, most things we have faith in are entirely possible. Although we would not need faith if we had certainty, faith need not be seen as the opposite to reason. We routinely believe that the Sun will rise tomorrow even though it might not. (→ 8) This is not a random belief conjured into existence out of thin air. It is one we have good reason to have faith in.

Everyday life therefore seems to present us with three basic options. Where certainty is available, we take it. Where certainty is not available we can take either the route of the ancient Sceptics and simply suspend judgement, or the faith route, in which case we make a judgement and hope for the best. In everyday terms, this is simply called 'making an assumption'. If we compare the suspension of judgement with making an assumption, making an assumption has one very considerable advantage: we can test an assumption and find out whether it is a good one or not. Faith opens the door to learning in a way that the suspension of judgement does not. ($\rightarrow$ 21)

Assuming the Sun will rise tomorrow is only the beginning of things. I assume that my breakfast will not poison me, I assume that my office is in the same place it was yesterday, I assume I can get to it by following the same route I took yesterday, and so on and so on. Our everyday lives are lived against the background of a whole raft of assumptions. There is nothing wrong in making assumptions, as long as we are aware that that is what we are doing. When Socrates engaged people in Athens in discussions of various topics with him, he revealed both to himself and them how little they actually knew and how much they were just assuming. They rarely found it an agreeable experience. The ancient Sceptics understood this. Their primary concern was not with how little people actually knew. What concerned them most was the suffering that comes from being attached to ideas that turn out to be unreliable.

In everyday life, assumptions can come in all shapes and sizes. If I am trying to solve a problem in algebra, for example, I may assume that '$x = 1$' and see how that works. If I get nowhere with that assumption, I may go back and try '$x = 2$', and so on. Similarly, if I am trying to crack a code I may assume that '$A = 1$' and so on. In such cases, assumptions are made in order to give me somewhere to begin in my attempt to solve the problem. I have no particular attachment to any such assumption and I am more than happy to jettison it if it turns out to be useless or incorrect. But even for mathematicians, these are not the typical assumptions we work with in everyday life.

Suppose I have to leave home at 8 each morning in order to be at work by 9. I assume that when my kitchen clock says it is 8 o'clock it actually is. If, one day, I leave home when the clock says 8, and nothing unusual happens on the way, but I find that it is 9.30 when I arrive at work, I may conclude that my clock is wrong. I can check this by checking my clock against another clock, or a time check on the radio, and so on. I might be accused of exaggeration if I say that my clock *made* me late for work, because I took the decision when to leave home, not the clock. (→ 10) But it would not be unreasonable to say that I was late *because of* the clock. My assumption that the clock was right guided my decision as to when to leave the house.

This is a relatively trivial example, but it shows how our assumptions guide and shape our decisions. Our assumption that the future will resemble the past guides our decision-making in a far more fundamental way. So do our wider assumptions concerning what the world is like. (→ 12) And so do our assumptions concerning what other people are like. (→ 15, 20) Over and over again in this book I have tried to show that we have options concerning what we do and do not believe. However, we can only make use of the ability to choose if we are aware that we have a choice. If I have been led to believe that it is an unchallengeable fact that human beings are fundamentally wicked, that belief will be in the background quietly shaping every interaction that I have with every human being. That is why I said at the beginning of this book that if you are not in control of your ideas, then they may be controlling you.

The assumption that my clock is telling the right time is easy to test. The assumption that human beings are fundamentally wicked is more difficult. The more basic and general our assumptions, the greater the role they play in shaping how we perceive the world. If I assume that human beings are fundamentally wicked, I will be sensitive to everything they do to confirm my assumption. When they act contrary to my assumption, I have a choice. I can either abandon (or at least refine) my assumption, or I can try to find a way of reconciling my assumption with my experience. The more deep-rooted the assumption, the more likely we are to take the second alternative. Why do some fundamentally wicked human beings do some things that are not wicked? Because they are afraid of being punished! Turned around and taken to a higher plane, this is an age-old theological problem: why does an omnipotent and benevolent god allow the presence of evil in the world?

The ancient Sceptics were not being unreasonable when they argued that there is very little, if anything, that we can be absolutely certain about. And the critics of Scepticism were not being unreasonable when they argued that absolute certainty was a much higher standard than we normally require for knowledge in everyday life. We are not being irrational if we choose to live *as if* we were absolutely certain that the Sun was going to rise tomorrow. We *are* being irrational if we argue that it is absolutely impossible that the Sun will not rise tomorrow. (→ 9) What we discover, if we pursue the examined life (→ 1) is that, in the realm of the 'as if', we are in control, because we can always choose another 'as if'. You can choose to live each day as if the world were going to end tomorrow. If we confuse the 'as if' with unalterable and unchallengeable facts, we are selling ourselves very short.

How would you live today if you thought the world was going to end tomorrow?

This is not a purely hypothetical question because every so often a movement emerges that manages to persuade its followers that the world is about to end. There have been hundreds of these, large and small, over the course of human history. No single pattern of behaviour is observable because it very much depends on what people believe will happen next. Is the end of the world the end of everything? Or is it the prelude to something better? And if so, for everyone or only for some?

There is nothing wrong in making assumptions, as long as we are in control of them. When we are not aware that we are making assumptions we may confuse how we *assume* things are with how things *really* are, and then our assumptions are in control of us. The worse the assumption is, the greater the damage that is done.

What would it take to persuade you that the Sun was not *going to rise tomorrow?*

I count our progress by the extent to which what we cried in the wilderness five and thirty years ago has now become part of the assumptions of the ordinary man and woman.

Clement Attlee

25. The examined life revisited

Philosophy is not a body of doctrine but an activity.
Ludwig Wittgenstein

Looking back and looking forward, what does this book tell you about philosophy and everyday life? And what will you do with it?

Whatever route you have taken through this book, by the time you get to this chapter you will have covered a lot of ground. Although this book is not a course in philosophy, you should by now have some understanding of what philosophy is about and how it relates to everyday life. Some of the topics you have encountered are very broad ones, for example what to believe (→ 2), fairness (→ 17) and language (→ 22). Others are narrower in scope, such as buying and selling (→ 13) and death (→ 23). This reflects the fact that in everyday life we are often applying general principles (→ 7) to specific situations and practices. We may always be trying to think straight (→ 4), but what we are trying to think straight *about* varies, sometimes even from minute to minute.

Above all, this book has given you things to *do*. The exercises, problems and questions that appear in every chapter are not add-on extras. They are absolutely central, because the examined life itself is something we do. As I pointed out at the beginning of this book

(→ Introduction), a lot of the time our lives are lived on a kind of mental autopilot. To some extent this is inevitable. Life is far too short to afford us the luxury of being able to endlessly agonize over every decision that has to be made in living our everyday lives. Learning skills, like driving a car, means that we can do numerous things 'without thinking', and that clearly has its practical advantages. But what if we have learnt to drive a car badly? Then there is a good chance that we will be involved in an accident and that can scarcely be in our best interests. What if our mental autopilot is steering us in the wrong direction? Then there is a good chance that we will not be successful in living the kind of life that we would like to. The examined life helps us to discover how our autopilot is programmed and, if necessary, reprogram it to help us get to where we really want to go. This is not a once-in-a-lifetime exercise. We have to be constantly on our guard against becoming less aware, forgetting why we believe what we do. We need to be constantly reflecting on our beliefs and, if necessary, updating them. The examined life involves developing new and good habits to replace old and bad ones.

If I had to boil this book down to its most basic elements, I would say that those elements consisted of two words, both of which are commands: 'Stop!' and 'Think!' Every chapter in this book invites you to stop and think about something or other. We have to stop in order to give ourselves time to reflect on what we are thinking, on what we are doing, on what we are saying, and why. The very act of reflection makes us immediately more aware of those things. Once we are aware, we can examine.

How do we examine? We can ask, 'Is this consistent?' (→ 7) We can ask, 'Is this logical?' (→ 4) We can ask, 'Should I believe this?' (→ 2) We can ask, 'Is this possible?' (→ 9) And so on. By examining we become more aware, better able to see how things are, and clearer about what options we have. Simply becoming aware that there *are* options is a fundamental step towards taking greater control of our lives.

None of this is easy, but no one ever accused Socrates of peddling a rest-cure. The examined life is hard work. Is it worth it? It would be difficult to argue that philosophy is in the business of delivering instant gratification, and perhaps sometimes ignorance really may be bliss. My own verdict would be that above everything else the examined life is about clarity. The clearer we are about who we are, what we are, what we want from life and how we are prepared to get it, the clearer our thinking, the clearer our understanding, the clearer our perception, the more likely we are to choose a good life and live the life of our choice. That may not be everything, but it is certainly something.

Printed in Great Britain
by Amazon

40351521R00097